# 1 INTERESTING FACT A DAY

366 INTERESTING FACTS FROM AROUND THE WORLD TO READ WITH THE FAMILY

SELECTION OF INTERESTING FACTS:
BUBBLES BOOKS

EDITING:
ROCÍO MACHUCA GARCÍA

GRAPHIC DESIGN & ILLUSTRATIONS:
SILVIA ROMA

TRANSLATION:
RHYS WESTON

# WELCOME TO THE INCREDIBLE WORLD OF INTERESTING FACTS!

AS OF NOW, IT'S TIME FOR THE OFFICIAL LAUNCH OF INTERESTING FACTS WITH THE FAMILY!
FOR EACH DAY OF THE YEAR, THERE IS ALREADY A SPECIAL MOMENT TO LEARN A NEW FACT.
CHILDREN WILL BE THE STARS OF THIS GREAT ADVENTURE, AS THEY GET NEW KNOWLEDGE ABOUT OUR PLANET, THE UNIVERSE, ANIMALS, AND THE HUMAN BODY.
ALL THIS WHILE THEY PRACTICE THEIR READING SKILLS AND DEVELOP THEIR READING COMPREHENSION.

ANY MOMENT IS A GOOD CHANCE TO LEARN SOMETHING NEW AND SURPRISING: FROM A BORING BREAKFAST IN THE MORNING TO A LONG TRIP IN THE CAR, TO GRANDMA'S BIRTHDAY PARTY, OR EVEN IN THE BEDROOM WITH OUR BROTHERS AND SISTERS.

EVEN IF THERE'S NO ONE TO TELL A SUPER INTERESTING FACT WE'VE JUST READ ABOUT, IT'S OK! WE CAN LAUGH ON OUR OWN AND TELL OTHER PEOPLE ABOUT ALL THE NEW THINGS WE'VE LEARNED ANOTHER TIME.

LISTEN UP SISTERS AND BROTHERS, GRANDMOTHERS AND GRANDFATHERS, MUMS AND DADS, UNCLES AND AUNTS, COUSINS, FRIENDS, CATS, AND DOGS... HERE IS OUR OFFICIAL INVITATION TO SHARE THESE FUN FACTS!

## 01 JANUARY

CAN YOU IMAGINE SPENDING 12 HOURS EATING NON-STOP? WELL, IF YOU WERE A PANDA BEAR, YOU WOULD DO THIS EVERY DAY! PANDAS NEED TO EAT LOTS AND LOTS OF BAMBOO TO GROW STRONG AND HEALTHY.

## 02 JANUARY

IF THERE WERE A SHERLOCK HOLMES IN THE ANIMAL WORLD, IT WOULD BE THE ELEPHANT. ELEPHANTS CAN FIND WATER WITHOUT SEEING IT AND FROM A LONG DISTANCE, AS FAR AS 155 MILES AWAY! THEY ARE ALSO VERY GOOD COMPANIONS BECAUSE IF ONE OF THEM FINDS WATER, THEY WILL LET THE OTHERS KNOW ABOUT IT.

## 03 JANUARY

WHICH IS HEAVIER, AN ELEPHANT OR A TONGUE? THIS DEPENDS ON WHICH TONGUE! WELL, WHEN IT COMES TO A BLUE WHALE, THE ANSWER IS... THE WHALE'S TONGUE!

**04** JANUARY

IF YOU PUT WHAT YOU HAVE EATEN DURING YOUR WHOLE LIFE ON A PLATE, IT WILL WEIGH THE SAME AS... 7 ELEPHANTS COMBINED!

**05** JANUARY

IF YOU WERE AN ANTEATER, YOU WOULD GET SICK OF EATING ANTS. THIS ANIMAL HAS NO TEETH, BUT ITS TONGUE IS SO LONG THAT IT CATCHES AS MANY AS 35,000 ANTS A DAY.

**06** JANUARY

IF YOU WERE THE MOTHER OF A PANDA BEAR, YOU'D CARRY IT IN THE PALM OF YOUR HAND... AS WHEN THEY'RE BORN, THEY'RE AS SMALL AS AN APPLE!

## 07 JANUARY

THERE ARE MANY WAYS TO MAKE 100% ECO-FRIENDLY PAPER, BUT SOME ARE MORE CREATIVE THAN OTHERS: IN SRI LANKA, A COUNTRY TO THE SOUTH OF INDIA, THERE IS A COMPANY THAT MAKES IT USING A VERY SPECIAL METHOD: THEY MIX RECYCLED PAPER WITH... ELEPHANT POOP!

## 08 JANUARY

IF I ASK YOU WHAT RABBITS EAT, YOU WILL PROBABLY SAY .... CARROTS! BUT DID YOU KNOW THAT THEY ALSO EAT THEIR OWN POOP? NOT JUST ANY POOP, THEY CHOOSE THE SOFTER POOP BECAUSE IT'S THE TASTIEST OF THEM ALL.

09 JANUARY

WHAT WOULD YOU NEED TO BUILD A VERY STRONG AND TOUGH HOUSE? IF YOU WANT TO USE THE OLDEST FORMULA, YOU WILL NEED WATER, GRASS, AND... COW POOP!

10 JANUARY

WHEN WE SNEEZE, WE BLOW OUT AIR AT A HIGH SPEED. IT'S SO QUICK THAT IT COULD OVERTAKE A CAR DRIVING AT 37 MILES PER HOUR.

11 JANUARY

CAN YOU IMAGINE HAVING HICCUPS FOR YEARS AND YEARS? THAT'S WHAT HAPPENED TO A MAN NAMED CHARLES OSBORNE, WHO HAD THEM FOR AS MANY AS... 69 YEARS OF HIS LIFE!

12 JANUARY

CAN YOU IMAGINE BEING AS HAIRY AS A CHIMPANZEE? BELIEVE IT OR NOT, WE ALL ARE! THE DIFFERENCE IS THAT WE DON'T SEE OUR BODY HAIR, BECAUSE MOST OF IT IS ALMOST INVISIBLE.

**13**
JANUARY

IF YOU WERE TO GO TO MARS, YOU WOULD LOSE A LOT OF WEIGHT! AND NOT BECAUSE OF THE JOURNEY, BUT DUE TO THE FORCE OF GRAVITY. TO FIND OUT HOW MUCH WOULD YOU WEIGH THERE, ALL YOU HAVE TO DO IS MULTIPLY YOUR WEIGHT BY 0.38. I WOULD LOSE 37KG (81 POUNDS) OF WEIGHT, WHAT ABOUT YOU?

**14**
JANUARY

ONCE UPON A TIME, TWO MOONS COLLIDED WITH EACH OTHER SO HARD THAT THE SMALLER ONE DISAPPEARED AND ONLY THE LARGER ONE REMAINED. WE DON'T KNOW IF THIS IS WHAT ACTUALLY HAPPENED, BUT THIS IS HOW THE EXPERTS EXPLAIN HOW THE DARK SIDE OF THE MOON IS ROUGH. .

**15**
JANUARY

IF WE LOOK AT THE NAMES OF THE PLANETS, WE CAN SEE THAT THEY ARE ALL NAMED AFTER ANCIENT GODS: MERCURY, VENUS, MARS, JUPITER, SATURN, URANUS, NEPTUNE... EXCEPT FOR EARTH, WHICH IS THE ONLY EXCEPTION. TIERRA, QUE ES LA ÚNICA EXCEPCIÓN.

## 16 JANUARY

GALAXIES ARE REALLY FAR AWAY. THE NEAREST ONE IS CALLED THE ANDROMEDA GALAXY, BUT EVEN IF YOU TRAVELLED AT THE SPEED OF LIGHT, IT WOULD TAKE YOU 2.5 MILLION YEARS TO GET THERE.

## 17 JANUARY

IF WE LIVED ON THE PLANETS JUPITER OR SATURN, WE'D BE RICH! BECAUSE OF THEIR ATMOSPHERIC AND CLIMATIC CONDITIONS, IT RAINS DIAMONDS ON THESE PLANETS!

## 18 JANUARY

HAVE YOU EVER WONDERED WHAT THE TEMPERATURE OF THE SUN IS? TO GIVE YOU AN IDEA, IF WATER BURNS WHEN IT BOILS AT 100 DEGREES CELCIUS (212 FARANHEIT), JUST IMAGINE HOW MUCH THE CORE OF THE SUN WOULD BURN AT OVER 15.7 MILLION DEGREES CELCIUS (28.2 MILLION FARANHEIT).

**19**
JANUARY

IF YOU THINK THAT ALL TOMATOES ARE RED AND ROUND, YOU ARE WRONG! THEY COME IN ALL COLOURS AND SHAPES: GREEN, YELLOW, BLACK, RECTANGULAR, OVAL, FLATTENED... UP TO 10,000 TYPES OF TOMATOES! SINCE THEY FIRST APPEARED IN THE ANCIENT AZTEC CULTURE, THEY HAVE CHANGED TO ADAPT TO ALL PARTS OF THE WORLD

**20**
JANUARY

WE KNOW THAT THE CARROT IS ORANGE, BUT IT WAS NOT ALWAYS LIKE THIS. MANY, MANY YEARS AGO IT WAS PURPLE ON THE OUTSIDE AND YELLOW ON THE INSIDE, THIS WAS BACK WHEN IT BEGAN TO BE GROWN IN A COUNTRY CALLED AFGHANISTAN IN ASIA.

**21**
JANUARY

DID YOU KNOW THAT IF YOU THROW AN APPLE INTO A JAR OF WATER IT FLOATS WITHOUT SINKING? THIS IS BECAUSE A QUARTER OF IT IS JUST AIR.

# 22
JANUARY

WHEN WE GO TO A SUPERMARKET, WE CAN BUY ALL KINDS OF SUGAR: WHITE, BROWN, COCONUT, POWDERED, GRANULATED... BUT IT WASN'T ALWAYS LIKE THIS. FOR EXAMPLE, IN THE MIDDLE AGES, ONLY THE VERY RICH COULD BUY SUGAR. IT WAS A REAL LUXURY PRODUCT BECAUSE OF THE HIGH PRICE THEY HAD TO PAY TO BRING IT FROM THE EAST.

# 23
JANUARY

DID YOU KNOW THAT HONEY IS THE ONLY FOOD THAT DOES NOT ROT? WE CAN KEEP IT FOR MANY YEARS IN OUR CUPBOARDS WITHOUT IT GOING OFF.

# 24
JANUARY

WE ALL LIKE TO EAT CHOCOLATE, BUT NOT AS MUCH AS THE PEOPLE OF SWITZERLAND. IN THIS COUNTRY, EACH PERSON EATS UP TO 10 KILOS A YEAR (22 POUNDS), WHICH IS EQUAL TO THE WEIGHT OF 5 MELONS.

**25** JANUARY

DID YOU KNOW THAT THE BIBLE IS THE WORLD'S BEST-SELLING BOOK? YOU COULD READ IT IN ALMOST ANY LANGUAGE, AS IT IS ALSO THE MOST TRANSLATED BOOK.

**26** JANUARY

THE BEST-SELLING NOVEL IN THE WORLD IS SPANISH AND IS CALLED DON QUIXOTE, WRITTEN BY MIGUEL DE CERVANTES.

**27** JANUARY

BELIEVE IT OR NOT, FRANKENSTEIN'S MONSTER WAS NOT CALLED FRANKENSTEIN! MARY SHELLEY, THE WOMAN WHO WROTE THE NOVEL, NEVER GAVE HIM A NAME. BUT ONE TIME WHEN SHE READ IT OUT IN FRONT OF AN AUDIENCE, SHE LET IT SLIP AND CALLED HIM "ADAM".

28
JANUARY

CAN YOU IMAGINE BEING AN ACTOR AND PLAYING SHERLOCK HOLMES? YOU WOULDN'T BE THE ONLY ONE TO PLAY THIS ROLE, AS WE ARE TALKING ABOUT THE MOST PORTRAYED CHARACTER IN HISTORY.

29
JANUARY

CAN YOU IMAGINE READING 1 MILLION WORDS? IF YOU READ ALL 7 HARRY POTTER BOOKS, YOU WILL HAVE DONE SO!

30
JANUARY

IF YOU LIKE READING COMICS, YOU NEED TO KNOW WHEN THEY WERE FIRST WRITTEN... HISTORIANS AGREE THAT THE FIRST COMIC BOOK IN HISTORY WAS THE "YELLOW KID", PUBLISHED IN 1895 IN A NEW YORK NEWSPAPER. THE COMIC WAS ABOUT A BOY WEARING YELLOW CLOTHES WITH WRITTEN TEXTS OF WHAT HE WANTED TO SAY.

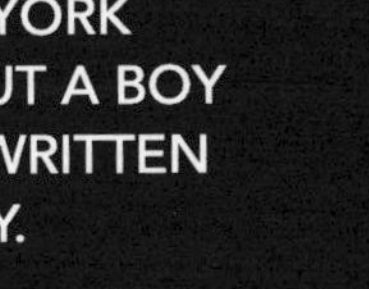

**31**
JANUARY

DID YOU KNOW THAT ALL OF US DROOL? WE MAKE SO MUCH SALIVA, WE COULD FILL A BOTTLE OF SALIVA EVERY DAY. AS A RESULT, WHAT WE EAT GETS SOFTER AND WE CAN SWALLOW IT WITHOUT IT HURTING US.

**01**
FEBRUARY

OUR INTESTINE IS SO LONG THAT WE COULD MAKE A ROPE OUT OF IT AND USE IT TO CLIMB DOWN FROM THE THIRD FLOOR OF A BUILDING.

**02**
FEBRUARY

IF YOU'RE MISSING A SCREW, THERE'S ALWAYS A SOLUTION: IF YOU PUT ALL THE IRON YOU CARRY IN YOUR BODY TOGETHER, YOU CAN MAKE A SCREW UP TO 7 CENTIMETRES LONG.

03
FEBRUARY

DID YOU KNOW THAT YOUR FOOT WILL ALWAYS BE THE SAME LENGTH AS THE DISTANCE BETWEEN YOUR ELBOW AND YOUR WRIST? IF YOU DON'T THINK THIS IS TRUE, PICK UP A SHOE AND TRY IT OUT!

04
FEBRUARY

YOU PROBABLY CUT YOUR TOENAILS LESS OFTEN THAN YOUR FINGERNAILS. THIS IS BECAUSE THEY TAKE UP TO FOUR TIMES LONGER TO GROW.

05
FEBRUARY

IF YOUR NOSE GROWS, IT'S NOT BECAUSE YOU'RE A LIAR. ACTUALLY, IT NEVER STOPS GROWING, AND NEITHER DO YOUR EARS! THE ONLY PART OF THE BODY THAT NEVER CHANGES IN SIZE FROM BIRTH IS YOUR EYES.

**06**
FEBRUARY

WE KNOW THAT MOUNT EVEREST IS ONE OF THE HIGHEST MOUNTAINS IN THE WORLD, BUT DID YOU KNOW THAT IT WILL GET HIGHER AND HIGHER? THIS IS BECAUSE IT IS ON TWO TECTONIC PLATES THAT FACE EACH OTHER AND PUSH THE MOUTAIN, CAUSING IT GROW BY 4 MILLIMETRES EVERY YEAR.

**07**
FEBRUARY

WHEN WE ARE AFRAID WE CRY OUT FOR HELP, AND BELIEVE IT OR NOT, SO DO PLANTS. THEY CAN'T CRY OUT FOR HELP, BUT THEY HAVE A CHEMICAL THAT MAKES THEIR SCENT STRONGER. SO WHEN THEY ARE ATTACKED BY A CATERPILLAR, THEY ATTRACT WASPS TO COME TO HELP THEM.

**08**
FEBRUARY

CAN YOU IMAGINE A FLOWER AS BIG AS AN UMBRELLA AND STINKING LIKE ROTTING MEAT? THIS IS THE RAFFLESIA AND IT IS FOUND IN THE AMAZON RAINFOREST. IT IS DEEP RED, AND IF YOU TOUCH IT, YOU WILL NOTICE THAT IT IS MEATY AND ROUGH.

**09**
FEBRUARY

YOU WOULD TAKE A VERY LONG TIME TO WALK AROUND THE WORLD'S BIGGEST TREE... IT'S 250 YEARS OLD AND AS BIG AS 3 FOOTBALL PITCHES! THIS IS THE BIG BANYAN TREE AND IT IS FOUND IN INDIA, VERY CLOSE TO KOLKATA.

**10**
FEBRUARY

IF YOU WALK THROUGH A FIELD OF SUNFLOWERS, YOU WILL NOTICE THAT THEY ALL FACE THE SUN. DURING THE DAY, THEY TURN FROM ONE SIDE TO THE OTHER TO FOLLOW THE SUNLIGHT, THAT'S THE REASON WHY THEY ARE CALLED SUNFLOWERS.

**11**
FEBRUARY

IF YOU WANT TO BUILD A TREE HOUSE, I DON'T RECOMMEND THE EUCALYPTUS: EVERY YEAR YOU WOULD NEED A LADDER 10 METRES (30 FEET) LONGER TO REACH THE TREE, WHICH CAN BE AS TALL AS AN 18-STOREY BUILDING.

**12** FEBRUARY

IF YOU CHOOSE A VERY COLD DAY TO GO ON A TRIP TO THE RIVER, YOU MAY BE LUCKY ENOUGH TO SEE WATER IN ALL ITS STAGES: WATER, ICE, AND STEAM. IN FACT, IN NATURE, WATER IS THE ONLY SUBSTANCE THAT CAN BE FOUND IN ALL FORMS: LIQUID, SOLID, AND GAS.

**13** FEBRUARY

DID YOU KNOW THAT MORE THAN HALF OF OUR BODY IS WATER? IF WE EMPTIED IT, WE COULD FILL UP TO 37 ONE-LITRE BOTTLES.

**14** FEBRUARY

THE PEOPLE OF HONG KONG ARE INTERESTING ! THEY PEE AND POOP IN THE SEAWATER, BUT NOT ON THE BEACH... INSTEAD IN THEIR TOILET! THEY DO THIS SO THAT THEY DON'T USE THE SMALL AMOUNT OF FRESHWATER THAT THEY HAVE.

15
FEBRUARY

BELIEVE IT OR NOT, YOU COULD GO WITHOUT EATING ANYTHING FOR UP TO A MONTH, BUT ONLY ONE WEEK WITHOUT DRINKING WATER.

16
FEBRUARY

YOU HAVE TO BE VERY CAREFUL WITH PETROL... NOT ONLY BECAUSE IT IS FLAMMABLE, BUT ALSO BECAUSE IT POLLUTES. A SINGLE DROP OF PETROL IS CAPABLE OF TURNING 25 LITRES OF DRINKING WATER INTO NON-DRINKING WATER.

17
FEBRUARY

DID YOU KNOW THAT A BOTTLE OF A FIZZY DRINK CAN HOLD 200 BOTTLES OF WATER? BELIEVE IT OR NOT, THIS IS THE AMOUNT OF WATER NEEDED TO MAKE THESE DRINKS.

**18** FEBRUARY

THE COLDEST PLACE ON THE PLANET IS NOT AT THE NORTH POLE... IT'S AT THE SOUTH POLE. IT'S CALLED ANTARCTICA, A HUGE CONTINENT OF ICE WHERE ON THE COLDEST DAYS IT REACHES MINUS 70 DEGREES CELSIUS (-94° FAHRENHEIT), AND ON THE WARMEST DAYS, MINUS 25 (-13° FAHRENHEIT)... STILL BELOW ZERO!

**19** FEBRUARY

DON'T TRY TO DRINK SEAWATER... UNLESS YOU ARE A PENGUIN! THANKS TO A SMALL GLAND IN THEIR BEAKS, PENGUINS HAVE THE INCREDIBLE ABILITY TO FILTER SALT WATER.

SO THAT THEY CAN DRINK GOOD WATER, THE GLAND GETS RID OF ALL THE CHLORINE, SODIUM, AND POTASSIUM THAT ARE NOT NEEDED.

**20** FEBRUARY

IF IT'S TOO COLD, IT'S BETTER TO STAY INDOORS... OR GO UNDERGROUND! THAT'S WHAT THEY DO IN CANADA AS THERE IS THE LARGEST UNDERGROUND CITY IN THE WORLD. PEOPLE DON'T LIVE THERE, BUT THEY CAN GO TO MORE THAN A THOUSAND SHOPS, BANKS, HAIRDRESSERS, BARS, AND RESTAURANTS.

21
FEBRUARY

PENGUINS ARE VERY NOBLE ANIMALS... BUT SOME ARE LITERALLY NOBLE! SUCH AS SIR NILS OLAV, WHO IS THE OFFICIAL MASCOT OF THE ROYAL GUARD IN NORWAY, AND THE APPOINTED SERGEANT, COLONEL, AND KNIGHT. NOW THAT'S A KING PENGUIN!

22
FEBRUARY

WOULD YOU DARE TO GO DOWN A HUGE ICE SLIDE? THIS IS HOW THE RUSSIANS HAD FUN MORE THAN 200 YEARS AGO WHEN THEY INVENTED THE FIRST ROLLER COASTER. 100 YEARS LATER, THE FRENCH CHANGED THE SLEDGES FOR CARRIAGES AND THE ICE FOR BIG WOODEN RAILS, TO BUILT THE ROLLER COASTER THAT WE ALL KNOW TODAY.

23
FEBRUARY

BELIEVE IT OR NOT, THE BIGGEST DESERT IN THE WORLD HAS NO SAND... BUT ICE! IT'S THE ANTARCTIC DESERT, WHERE IT DOESN'T RAIN, AND ONLY PENGUINS, SEALS, SEAGULLS, AND SEA LIONS LIVE THERE.

24
FEBRUARY

IF YOU WANT TO DRAW THE FLAG OF A COUNTRY AND USE THE COLOUR PURPLE, YOU HAVE ONLY TWO OPTIONS: NICARAGUA, TO DRAW A RAINBOW IN THE CENTRE OF THE FLAG, AND THE DOMINICA, TO COLOUR IN THE FEATHERS OF A PARROT.

25
FEBRUARY

IF YOU WANT TO KNOW WHAT THE COLOURS OF THE ITALIAN FLAG ARE, ORDER A MARGHERITA PIZZA! THE ITALIANS INVENTED IT MORE THAN 100 YEARS AGO FOR QUEEN MARGHERITA, WITH THE INGREDIENTS REPRESENTING THE COLOURS: BASIL FOR GREEN, CHEESE FOR WHITE, AND TOMATO FOR RED.

26
FEBRUARY

IF YOU THOUGHT THAT ALL FLAGS ARE RECTANGULAR, YOU'RE WRONG! THERE ARE ALSO SQUARE ONES, BUT ONLY IN TWO COUNTRIES: SWITZERLAND AND VATICAN CITY.

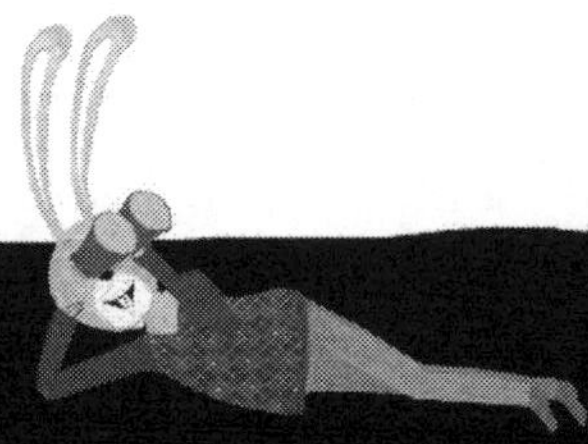

27
FEBRUARY

A FLAG THAT IS REALLY COOL IS THAT OF... PARAGUAY! IT'S THE ONLY FLAG IN THE WORLD WITH TWO SIDES AND A DIFFERENT DESIGN ON EACH SIDE. THEY ARE THE SYMBOLS OF THE REPUBLIC AND THE TREASURY, INVENTED BY A MAN CALLED GASPAR RODRIGUEZ DE FRANCIA.

28
FEBRUARY

HAVE YOU EVER WONDERED HOW MANY RAYS THE SUN HAS? IF YOU ASK AN ARGENTINE OR AN URUGUAYAN, FOR EXAMPLE, YOU WON'T BE SO SURE! BOTH OF THESE COUNTRIES HAVE INCA SUN GOD ON THEIR FLAGS, BUT ONE HAS 32 RAYS AND THE OTHER WITH 26.

29
FEBRUARY

DO YOU KNOW WHICH COUNTRY HAS CHANGED ITS FLAG THE MOST TIMES THROUGHOUT HISTORY? IT IS AFGHANISTAN, WHICH HAS CHANGED ITS FLAG 15 TIMES. HOWEVER, IT HAS ALWAYS KEPT ITS EMBLEM AND ONLY CHANGED THE DESIGN OF THE FLAG.

**01**
MARCH

WHAT IS THE MOST AQUATIC ANIMAL IN THE WORLD? IF YOUR ANSWER IS THE DOLPHIN OR THE WHALE, YOU'RE WRONG! IT IS THE JELLYFISH, AN ANIMAL MADE UP OF 95% WATER.

**02**
MARCH

IF PEOPLE FILTER WATER TO MAKE IT CLEANER, SO DO FISH! THEY DON'T DO IT WITH A JUG OR A TAP (OF COURSE NOT!), BUT WITH THEIR GILLS, WHICH REMOVE THE SALT.

**03**
MARCH

IF YOU TRY TO CATCH A FISH, YOU ARE UNLIKELY TO BE ABLE TO. ESPECIALLY SAILFISHES: THEY RUN FASTER THAN A CAR ON THE MOTORWAY, SWIMMING AT A SPEED OF 68 MILES PER HOUR.

04
MARCH

IF YOU TRY TO KILL A SCORPION, IT MIGHT EVEN BEAT YOU TO IT. THIS IS THE ONLY ANIMAL IN THE WORLD THAT, WHEN IT FEELS THREATENED, KILLS ITSELF BEFORE IT IS ATTACKED.

05
MARCH

CAN YOU IMAGINE HAVING TO BRUSH 3,000 TEETH? THAT WOULD TAKE A LOT OF TIME! BELIEVE IT OR NOT, THERE IS AN ANIMAL THAT HAS THIS NUMBER OF TEETH... AND THEY CAN BE UP TO 7 CENTIMETRES LONG! THIS IS THE GREAT WHITE SHARK.

06
MARCH

CLOWNFISH IS NOT GOOD AT LAUGHING, BUT THEY ARE GOOD AT TAKING CARE OF THEIR YOUNG. THIS FISH HAS A UNIQUE ABILITY TO TRANSFORM ITSELF INTO A FEMALE TO TAKE CARE OF ITS OFFSPRING WHEN THE MOTHER FISH ABANDONS THEM.

**07** MARCH

WHEN WE THINK OF A PILLOW, WE IMAGINE A SOFT AND FLUFFY CUSHION. BUT IT WASN'T ALWAYS LIKE THAT, QUITE THE OPPOSITE: IN MESOPOTAMIA, THE FIRST PILLOWS WERE MADE OF STONE AND WERE USED TO KEEP INSECTS AWAY FROM PEOPLE'S MOUTHS, NOSES, AND EARS.

**08** MARCH

ONCE UPON A TIME THERE WAS A MAN THAT WAS SO TALL... THAT HE COULD NOT FIT THROUGH THE DOOR OF HIS HOUSE AND EVEN WHEN HE WAS INSIDE IT, ALL HE COULD DO WAS SIT DOWN. ALTHOUGH WE DON'T KNOW HOW IT ACTUALLY WAS FOR THE WORLD'S TALLEST MAN CALLED ROBERT WADLOW, WHO WAS 8 FEET AND 11.1 INCHES TALL (2.72 METRES), BUT WE CAN ONLY IMAGINE HOW IT WAS.

**09** MARCH

BELIEVE IT OR NOT, IN ANCIENT TIMES PEOPLE WERE ABLE TO LIVE WITHOUT MOBILE PHONES... BUT NOT WITHOUT TOILET PAPER. THE FIRST TO USE IT WERE THE CHINESE, ALMOST 2,000 YEARS AGO!

**10** MARCH

IF I TELL YOU CHIN CHAN PU, PIKACHÚ, CACHIPÚN, JANKENPÓN, YAN KEN PO, PIN PON PAPAS OR KAKEMBÓ, YOU PROBABLY DON'T KNOW WHAT I'M TALKING ABOUT... BUT WHAT ABOUT IF I SAID ROCK, PAPER OR SCISSORS? THESE ARE JUST SOME OF THE NAMES OF THIS FAMOUS GAME, KNOWN AND TRANSLATED ALL OVER THE WORLD SINCE IT WAS INVENTED IN CHINA.

11 MARCH

CAN YOU IMAGINE SKIING WITH A WOODEN STICK? THIS IS WHAT THE RUSSIANS DID 8,000 YEARS AGO. EVEN THOUGH IT MIGHT SEEM LIKE A MODERN HOBBY, IN ANCIENT TIMES IT WAS A VERY USEFUL AND NECESSARY FORM OF TRANSPORT TO GLIDE OVER THE SNOW.

12 MARCH

DID YOU KNOW THAT THE OLDEST TOY WASN'T REALLY A TOY AT ALL? MORE THAN 5,000 YEARS AGO, MESOPOTAMIAN CHILDREN DID NOT PLAY WITH PLAY DOUGH OR DOLLS... BUT WITH ANIMAL BONES!

13 MARCH

WHICH PART OF YOUR BODY DO YOU MOVE THE MOST DURING THE DAY? IT'S NOT YOUR LEGS OR YOUR FEET: IT'S YOUR EYES, AND YOU PROBABLY MOVE THEM MUCH MORE THAN YOU THINK... UP TO 100,000 TIMES A DAY!

14 MARCH

HAVE YOU EVER NOTICED THAT WHEN YOU SNEEZE YOU ALWAYS CLOSE YOUR EYES? BUT IT'S NOT YOU WHO CLOSES THEM, BUT YOUR BRAIN. IT DOES THIS TO PROTECT YOUR EYES FROM GETTING INFECTED BY THE MICRO-ORGANISMS THAT COME OUT OF YOUR MOUTH.

15 MARCH

CATS ARE TRUE MAGICIANS! THANKS TO THEIR NIGHT VISION, THEY MAKE THE INVISIBLE VISIBLE! UNLIKE PEOPLE, CATS SEE LESS DURING THE DAY BUT UP TO 7 TIMES MORE AT NIGHT.

**16**
**MARCH**

CAN YOU IMAGINE AN EYE AS BIG AS A CAR WHEEL? THE GIANT SQUID HAS THE LARGEST EYES IN THE WORLD THAT ARE 38 CENTIMETRES (15 INCHES) IN SIZE.

**17**
**MARCH**

HAVE YOU EVER TRIED SLEEPING WITH YOUR EYES OPEN? YOU'LL NEVER BE ABLE TO... UNLESS YOU'RE A SNAKE! SNAKES DON'T HAVE SUPERPOWERS, BUT THEY DO HAVE VERY SPECIAL EYES: AS THEY HAVE NO EYELIDS, THEY KEEP THEM OPEN THROUGHOUT THEIR ENTIRE LIVES.

**18**
**MARCH**

WHEN YOU SEE A FROG OR TOAD CLOSE ITS EYES, IT'S NOT BECAUSE THEY DOESN'T WANT TO SEE YOU. ACTUALLY, THEY DO THIS SO THEY CAN SWALLOW FOOD THEY EAT WHOLE, AS THEY CAN'T CHEW BECAUSE THEY DO NOT HAVE ANY TEETH.

19
MARCH

THE TASMANIAN DEVIL IS NOT A DEVIL, BUT IT IS A BIG EATER. IN JUST HALF AN HOUR, THIS ANIMAL IS CAPABLE OF EATING AS MUCH AS HALF ITS OWN WEIGHT.

20
MARCH

IF A HYENA SMILES AT YOU, DON'T TRUST IT: WITH ITS POWERFUL STOMACH AND STRONG JAWS, IT CAN EAT AN ENTIRE ANIMAL AND NOT EVEN LEAVE ITS SKIN, TEETH, HORNS, AND BONES BEHIND.

21
MARCH

CAN YOU IMAGINE IF YOUR SKIN WAS THE SAME COLOUR AS THE FOOD YOU EAT? THIS IS WHAT HAPPENS TO FLAMINGOS, WHICH ARE BORN WITH WHITE OR GREY FEATHERS, BUT AS THEY GROW UP THEY CHANGE TO THE PINK OR ORANGE COLOUR CAUSED BY THE BUGS THEY EAT.

22
MARCH

GREAT WHITE SHARKS EAT AN AVERAGE OF 11,000 KILOS OF FOOD A YEAR, BUT THEY DON'T ALWAYS EAT EVERY DAY. THIS LARGE FISH CAN GO UP TO 3 MONTHS WITHOUT EATING ANY FOOD.

23
MARCH

HAVE YOU EVER NOTICED HOW FLIES EAT? IF YOU LOOK, IT IS AS IF THEY DRINK THROUGH A STRAW! THIS IS BECAUSE THEY HAVE NO TEETH, SO THEY CAN ONLY DRINK TO FEED THEMSELVES.

24
MARCH

DID YOU KNOW THAT IN AN AEROPLANE, THE PILOT AND CO-PILOT ALWAYS CHOOSE DIFFERENT MEALS? AND NOT BECAUSE THEY WANT TO, BUT BECAUSE IF ONE OF THE MEALS IS IN A ROTTEN STATE, THEN ONE OF THEM WILL STILL BE ABLE TO FLY.

**25** MARCH

SPRING AND SUMMER MAKE US VERY HAPPY, BUT DID YOU KNOW THAT THEY ALSO MAKE YOU GROW TALLER? THIS IS BECAUSE YOU GET MORE SUN, MORE SLEEP, AND MOVE AROUND MORE.

**26** MARCH

HOW MANY INSECTS ARE THERE IN THE WORLD? SO MANY! IT IS ESTIMATED THAT THERE ARE 200 MILLION INSECTS FOR EVERY HUMAN BEING. WOULD YOU BE SO BRAVE AS TO CALCULATE THIS?

**27** MARCH

CAN YOU IMAGINE IF YOUR TEETH NEVER STOPPED GROWING? ALTHOUGH IT MAY SEEM HARD TO BELIEVE, THIS IS WHAT HAPPENS TO HORSES. THIS IS BECAUSE IT TAKES A GOOD SET OF TEETH TO CHEW ALL THE GRASS THAT THEY EAT FOR 12 HOURS A DAY.

## 28 MARCH

ONCE UPON A TIME THERE WAS SOMEONE WITH SUCH LONG HAIR... THAT IT COULD GO FROM MADRID TO BARCELONA! THIS MAY SEEM IMPOSSIBLE, BUT IF YOU NEVER CUT YOUR HAIR, YOU COULD GROW IT EVEN MORE, WITH HAIR UP TO 450 MILES LONG.

## 29 MARCH

IF THEY ALWAYS SAY TO YOU: YOU'VE GROWN SO MUCH! YOU'RE SO BIG! IMAGINE WHAT THEY WOULD SAY IF YOU WERE A BAMBOO DRAGON, A PLANT THAT GROWS 4 CENTIMETRES (1.5 INCHES) EVERY DAY.

## 30 MARCH

WHICH GROWS FASTER, YOUR NAILS OR YOUR MOUSTACHE? BELIEVE IT OR NOT (AND YOU CAN'T EVEN SEE IT), FACIAL HAIR IS THE FASTEST-GROWING PART OF YOUR BODY.

31
MARCH

THE CANARY PINE IS A SUPERHERO! WITH ITS INDESTRUCTIBLE SKIN, IT IS THE ONLY TREE CAPABLE OF BEING REBORN AFTER BURNING IN A FIRE.

01
APRIL

NOBODY HAS A TONGUE LIKE YOURS... AND EVERYONE'S IS DIFFERENT! IF YOU LOOK CLOSELY, YOU WILL SEE THAT EACH TONGUE HAS ITS OWN UNIQUE AND INDIVIDUAL PRINT, JUST LIKE THOSE FOUND ON OUR FINGERTIPS.

02
APRIL

DO YOU KNOW HOW ONE CAT IS DIFFERENT FROM THE OTHERS? WE MIGHT SAY BECAUSE OF THE COLOUR OF ITS FUR OR THE SIZE OF ITS EARS, BUT WHAT MAKES A CAT UNIQUE IS ITS LITTLE NOSE: IT IS LIKE THEIR FINGERPRINT AND THEIR IDENTITY, YOU WILL NEVER FIND TWO OF THEM THE SAME!

**03 APRIL**

KOALAS LOOK A LOT MORE LIKE US THAN YOU MIGHT THINK. IT'S NOT BECAUSE THEY EAT EUCALYPTUS LEAVES OR SLEEP ON TREE BRANCHES, BUT BECAUSE OF THEIR FINGERPRINTS, WHICH ARE CLOSE TO THOSE OF HUMANS.

**04 APRIL**

YOUR SMELL IS UNIQUE AND WILL NEVER BE THE SAME AS SOMEONE ELSE'S... EXCEPT IF YOU HAVE A TWIN SIBLING!

**05 APRIL**

PEOPLE CAN BE PHYSICALLY VERY DIFFERENT, AND EVEN THOUGH AT FIRST GLANCE IT MAY NOT SEEM SO, AND THIS IS THE SAME FOR ZEBRAS. THERE ARE NOT BLONDES AND BRUNETTES OR BLUE EYES AND BROWN EYES, BUT THEY DO HAVE A PATTERN THAT MAKES THEM DIFFERENT AND UNIQUE. THEY USE THEIR PATTERNS TO RECOGNISE EACH OTHER AND FIND OTHERS IN A GROUP.

06

APRIL

HAVE YOU EVER NOTICED HOW MANY GRAINS A COB OF CORN HAS? IF YOU COUNT THEM, YOU WILL FIND THAT THEY WILL ALWAYS HAVE AN EVEN NUMBER.

07

APRIL

WE DON'T USUALLY LIKE FLIES, BUT DID YOU KNOW THAT THANKS TO THEM WE CAN EAT CHOCOLATE? THIS IS BECAUSE OF A FLY CALLED THE MIDGE, WHICH FEEDS THE COCOA PLANT THAT GIVES US CHOCOLATE.

08

APRIL

CHOCOLATE BONBONS ARE NOT GOOD, THEY'RE DELICIOUS! MAYBE THAT'S WHY THE FRENCH CALLED THEM "BON BON", WHICH MEANS "TWICE AS GOOD".

**09** APRIL

IF YOU WANT TO MAKE THE WORLD'S BIGGEST PIZZA, YOU WILL NEED AT LEAST: 3,600 KILOS (7,936 POUNS) OF DOUGH, 1,600 KILOS (3,527 POUNDS) OF CHEESE, AND 2,500 KILOS (5,511 POUNDS) OF TOMATO SAUCE. THAT'S WHAT THEY USED IN CALIFORNIA TO MAKE THE LONGEST PIZZA IN HISTORY, 2 KILOMETRES (1.24 MILES) LONG AND WEIGHING 8,000 KILOS (17,638 POUNDS).

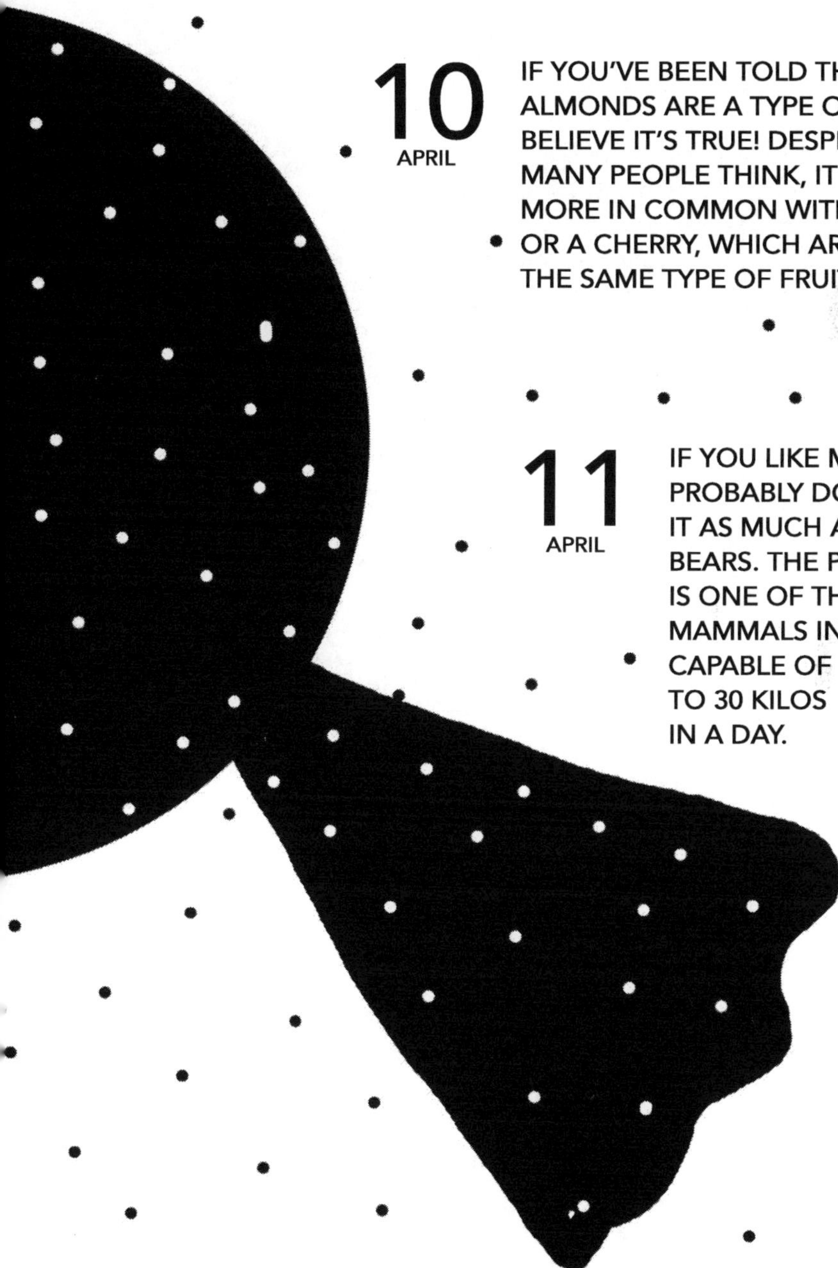

**10** APRIL

IF YOU'VE BEEN TOLD THAT ALMONDS ARE A TYPE OF NUT, DON'T BELIEVE IT'S TRUE! DESPITE WHAT MANY PEOPLE THINK, IT HAS MUCH MORE IN COMMON WITH AN OLIVE OR A CHERRY, WHICH ARE ACTUALLY THE SAME TYPE OF FRUIT.

**11** APRIL

IF YOU LIKE MEAT, YOU PROBABLY DON'T LIKE IT AS MUCH AS POLAR BEARS. THE POLAR BEAR IS ONE OF THE LARGEST MAMMALS IN THE WORLD, CAPABLE OF EATING UP TO 30 KILOS (66 POUNDS) IN A DAY.

**12** APRIL

DID YOU KNOW THAT THE OCEAN WAS A GOD CALLED OCEANUS AND THE FATHER OF ALMOST 3,000 GODS? ŌKEANOS, WHICH IS THE ORIGINAL WORD, COMES FROM GREEK MYTHOLOGY AND WAS USED TO DESCRIBE A "GREAT CURRENT THAT GOES AROUND THE DISC OF THE EARTH."

**13** APRIL

YOU WOULD HAVE TO BE REALLY BIG TO BE ONE OF THE SMALLEST OCEANS IN THE WORLD. THE ARCTIC OCEAN COVERS AN AREA OF ABOUT 8.7 MILLION SQUARE MILES AND CIRCLES THE NORTH POLE, COVERING NORTHERN EUROPE, ASIA, AND THE AMERICAS.

**14** APRIL

WHAT COLOUR IS SAND? DID YOU KNOW THAT THERE IS ALSO GREEN SAND? A PRECIOUS VOLCANIC MINERAL CALLED OLIVINE MAKES IT THAT COLOUR, BUT THERE ARE ONLY 4 PLACES IN THE WORLD WHERE IT CAN BE FOUND:

- PAPAKOLEA BEACH, HAWAII
- TALOFOFO BEACH, ON THE ISLAND OF GUAM
- CORMORANT POINT, IN THE GALAPAGOS ISLANDS
- HORNINDALSVATNET LAKE, NORWAY

**15** APRIL

WHEN WE THINK OF CANADA, WE THINK OF BEARS AND COLD. BUT DID YOU KNOW THAT IT IS ALSO THE COUNTRY WITH THE MOST LAKES ON EARTH? IN TOTAL, THERE ARE MORE THAN 32,000 LAKES, WHICH IS MORE THAN HALF OF ALL THE LAKES IN THE WORLD!

**16** APRIL

WOULD YOU WANT TO SWIM IN THE LARGEST SWIMMING POOL IN THE WORLD? YOU WOULD NEED TO SWIM MORE THAN HALF A MILE AND DIVE DOWN 3,5 METRES (11,5 FEET) TO GET TO THE BOTTOM. BUT TO FIND IT, YOU WOULD HAVE TO TRAVEL ALL THE WAY TO CHILE, TO A TOWN CALLED ALGARROBO.

**17** APRIL

CAN YOU “PLAY DEAD” TO FLOAT IN THE WATER? MAYBE YOU ARE ONE OF THE FEW WHO CAN DO IT, BUT IN CHILE THERE IS A PLACE WHERE EVERYONE CAN DO IT: THE CEJAR LAGOON, A SALTWATER LAGOON WHERE EVERYONE FLOATS WITHOUT SINKING BECAUSE THERE IS A LARGE AMOUNT OF SALT IN THE WATER.

18 APRIL

FOOD HAS AN EXPIRY DATE... AND SO DOES THE PLANET WE LIVE ON. MANY YEARS FROM NOW IT IS PREDICTED THAT THE MILKY WAY AND OUR GALAXY WILL COLLIDE WITH ANOTHER GALAXY CALLED ANDROMEDA. BUT THERE IS NO NEED TO WORRY NOW AS IF THIS EVER HAPPENS, IT WILL BE IN 4 BILLION YEARS.

19 APRIL

CAN YOU IMAGINE A SKY THAT IS RED IN THE DAYTIME AND BLUE DURING SUNSET? THE SKY ON MARS IS LIKE THIS, WITH COLOURS THAT ACT IN THE OPPOSITE WAY TO OUR PLANET.

20 APRIL

THE ASTRONAUTS WHO LANDED ON THE MOON 50 YEARS AGO HAVE LEFT A TRACE THAT WILL LAST FOREVER. THIS IS VERY QUITE LITERALLY TRUE BECAUSE THERE IS NO WIND OR RAIN TO TAKE THEM AWAY FROM THERE, SO THEY WILL STAY THERE FOREVER.

**21** APRIL

YOU WOULD NEVER STOP COUNTING ALL THE STARS IN THE SKY... THERE ARE BETWEEN 100,000 AND 400,000 STARS IN OUR GALAXY, AND THE SUN IS ONLY ONE OF THEM. WE ONLY HAVE ONE MOON, BUT ON SOME PLANETS THERE ARE SEVERAL: 70 ON JUPITER AND 81 ON SATURN.

**22** APRIL

LIKE THE EARTH, ALL PLANETS REVOLVE AROUND THEMSELVES. BUT DID YOU KNOW THAT VENUS AND URANUS ARE THE ONLY ONES THAT ROTATE IN THE OPPOSITE DIRECTION TO THE OTHER PLANETS?

**23** APRIL

THE FIRST PERSON TO TRAVEL AROUND THE WORLD WAS 500 YEARS AGO, A SPANISH NAVIGATOR NAMED JUAN SEBASTIAN DE ELCANO. IT TOOK HIM THREE YEARS TO SAIL AROUND THE WORLD AND RETURN TO THE STARTING PORT.

24 APRIL

THE STATUE OF LIBERTY HAS CHANGED COLOUR! THIS IS NOT DUE TO A GENIUS PAINTER, NEITHER FROM ONE DAY TO THE NEXT... BUT TIME AND AIR POLLUTION HAVE CHANGED THE REDDISH COLOUR THAT IT HAD WHEN IT WAS BUILT, TO THE GREEN COLOUR THAT WE ALL SEE TODAY.

25 APRIL

WHO DISCOVERED AMERICA? IF YOUR ANSWER IS CHRISTOPHER COLUMBUS, YOU'RE WRONG! IT WAS ACTUALLY THE VIKINGS, 500 YEARS BEFORE IT WAS DISCOVERED BY COLUMBUS. THIS IS PROVEN BY THE REMAINS OF HOUSES AND OTHER OBJECTS FOUND THERE, ON A LAND THEY CALLED VINLAND, WHERE THEY LIVED FOR ABOUT 20 YEARS.

26 APRIL

THERE IS NO ARMY IN COSTA RICA: MORE THAN 70 YEARS BACK, IN 1948, THIS COUNTRY TRADED ITS SOLDIERS FOR EDUCATION, CULTURE, AND NATIONAL SECURITY.

27 APRIL

THE OLDEST UNIVERSITY IN THE WORLD IS ALMOST 800 YEARS OLD. THIS IS OXFORD UNIVERSITY, WHICH WAS FOUNDED IN 1249.

28
APRIL

MORE THAN 130 YEARS AGO, ONLY MEN WERE ALLOWED TO VOTE IN EVERY COUNTRY IN THE WORLD. WOMEN HAD TO STRUGGLE UNTIL 1893 WHEN WOMEN IN NEW ZEALAND WON THE RIGHT TO VOTE FOR THE FIRST TIME THANKS TO A WOMAN NAMED KATE SHEPPARD.

29
APRIL

DID YOU KNOW THAT THERE WERE NO ALARM CLOCKS MORE THAN 200 YEARS AGO? IN IRELAND AND ENGLAND, ALARM CLOCKS WERE PEOPLE! THEY WERE CALLED " KNOCKER UPS" AND THEIR JOB WAS TO WAKE UP THE WORKERS IN THE FACTORIES SO THAT THEY COULD GET TO THEIR JOBS ON TIME.

**30** APRIL

DID YOU KNOW THAT MICE AND RATS LAUGH WHEN YOU TICKLE THEM? YOU SHOULDN'T TRY THIS AS THEY MIGHT BITE YOU... BUT IF YOU DID, YOU'D SEE HOW MUCH FUN THEY HAVE WITH YOUR HAND.

**01** MAY

CAN YOU IMAGINE EATING WITHOUT HAVING A STOMACH? WELL, THIS IS HOW IT IS FOR THE PLATYPUS, WHICH DOES NOT HAVE A STOMACH AS ITS THROAT CARRIES FOOD STRAIGHT TO ITS INTESTINES.

**02** MAY

DID YOU KNOW THAT A DOG CAN UNDERSTAND YOU WHEN YOU SPEAK TO IT? IT CAN TELL THE DIFFERENCE BETWEEN A FAMILIAR AND AN UNFAMILIAR LANGUAGE, AND EVEN KNOW THE DIFFERENCE BETWEEN EVERYDAY SPEECH AND A SENTENCE WITHOUT ANY MEANING.

03 MAY

IF YOU ARE AFRAID OF BATS, NEVER GO NEAR BRACKEN BAT CAVE IN TEXAS. EVERY YEAR BETWEEN MARCH AND OCTOBER, AROUND 20 MILLION FREE-TAILED BATS SETTLE THERE, WHICH MAKES IT NOT ONLY THE LARGEST COLONY OF BATS BUT POSSIBLY THE LARGEST GATHERING OF MAMMALS IN THE WORLD.

04 MAY

WATCH OUT FOR BEES, BECAUSE ONE DAY THEY MIGHT RECOGNISE YOU! BEES CAN SEE SO WELL AND ARE SO SMART THAT IF THEY WERE TRAINED THEY COULD EVEN BE ABLE TO RECOGNISE OUR FACES. THIS IS BECAUSE LIKE PEOPLE, THEY DON'T JUST SEE MOUTHS AND NOSES SEPARATELY, BUT THE FACE AS A WHOLE.

05 MAY

IF THERE IS AN ANIMAL OF FEW WORDS, IT WOULD BE THE GIRAFFE. IN FACT, GIRAFFES ARE COMPLETELY SILENT, BEING THE ONLY MAMMAL THAT HAS NO VOCAL CORDS.

## 06 MAY

DID YOU KNOW THAT THERE IS AN ANIMAL OLDER THAN TREES? SHARKS WERE HERE EVEN BEFORE THE DINOSAURS, MORE THAN 400 MILLION YEARS AGO.

## 07 MAY

NO MATTER HOW MUCH WE SAY SO, WE ARE UNLIKELY TO FIND ANYTHING THAT IS “OLDER THAN METHUSELAH”. YOU WOULD NEED TO BE INCREBILY OLD TO BE OLDER THAN THIS ANCIENT TREE, WHICH IS THE OLDEST TREE IN THE WORLD THAT IS AROUND 5,000 YEARS OLD.

## 08 MAY

PLANTS GIVE US BEAUTIFUL FLOWERS, BUT THEY CAN ALSO TEACH US VERY VALUABLE THINGS. WHEN THEY ARE THE SAME KIND OF SPECIES, THEY TAKE GREAT CARE OF EACH OTHER: PLANTS ADAPT THEIR GROWTH TO THE SPACE THEY SHARE WITH THEIR RELATIVES, LEAVING ENOUGH ROOM AND LIGHT FOR ALL OF THEM.

09
MAY

DID YOU KNOW THAT IF WE RECYCLED ALL OF THE NEWSPAPERS IN THE WORLD, WE WOULD SAVE MORE THAN 250 MILLION TREES EVERY YEAR?

10
MAY

DID YOU KNOW THAT CARNIVOROUS PLANTS DON'T EAT MEAT? DESPITE WHAT THEIR NAME MAY SUGGEST, THEY ONLY EAT INSECTS AND NOT JUST ANY INSECT: THERE IS A MECHANISM THAT SEPARATES THE STEM FROM THE TRAP THAT THEY USE FOR FOOD, SO THEY CAN TELL THE DIFFERENCE BETWEEN THE INSECTS USED FOR FOOD AND THOSE THAT POLLINATE THEM SO THAT THEY CAN REPRODUCE.

11
MAY

TO REACH THE TOP OF THE TALLEST TREE IN THE WORLD, YOU WOULD NEED TO CLIMB UP BIG BEN AND THEN KEEP GOING UP 7 MORE FLOORS: WITH A HEIGHT OF 115 METRES (377 FEET) AND AN APPROXIMATE AGE OF 600 YEARS, IT IS NO COINCIDENCE THAT WE CALL IT HYPERION, WHO WAS THE TITAN GOD OF HEAVENLY LIGHTY IN GREEK MYTHOLOGY.

**12** MAY

IF YOU THROW AWAY A GLASS BOTTLE IT WILL TAKE MORE THAN 4,000 YEARS TO DISAPPEAR.

**13** MAY

ALUMINIUM CANS CAN COME IN ALL SHAPES AND SIZES AND CAN LIVE FOREVER! WE RECYCLE THIS MATERIAL, AGAIN AND AGAIN, TO GIVE IT A NEW LIFE IN JUST 2 MONTHS. IF YOU THINK ABOUT IT, IT'S JUST LIKE BUYING THE SAME CAN OF TOMATOES, AFTER THROWING IT AWAY MONTHS BEFORE.

**14** MAY

WE CAN LEARN A LOT FROM FINLANDERS, WHERE 9 OUT OF 10 PLASTIC BOTTLES AND ALMOST 100% OF GLASS BOTTLES ARE RECYCLED.

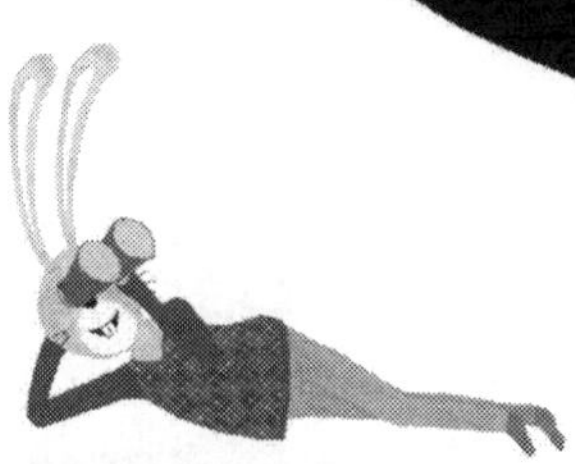

15 MAY

RECYCLING ALSO SAVES A LOT OF ENERGY: THE SAME ENERGY THAT IS USED TO MAKE 1 NEW METAL CAN IS ENOUGH TO MAKE UP TO 20 RECYCLED ONES.

16 MAY

IF YOU RECYCLE 1 TONNE OF PAPER YOU WILL SAVE THE LIFE OF 22 TREES, AS WELL AS SAVING 71% OF ELECTRICITY AND YOU WILL HAVE MUCH CLEANER AIR, WITH 74% LESS POLLUTION.

17 MAY

WE WOULD NEED ALMOST 5 PLANETS LIKE OURS IF WE ALL WANTED TO KEEP LIVING THE WAY PEOPLE IN THE UNITED STATES DO.

18 MAY

DID YOU KNOW THAT THE FAMOUS EIFFEL TOWER HIDES A BIG SECRET? THERE IS A 90-SQUARE-METRE HOUSE INSIDE IT WHICH THE DESIGNER GUSTAVE EIFFEL HAD BUILT FOR HIMSELF, AND IT IS 280 METRES (918 FEET) HIGH!

19 MAY

TODAY WE ALL KNOW ABOUT THE EIFFEL TOWER IN PARIS, BUT DID YOU THAT IT COULD HAVE BEEN BUILT IN BARCELONA BEFORE THAT? THE EIFFEL TOWER WAS BUILT FOR THE 1888 WORLD EXHIBITION, BUT IT WAS REJECTED BY BARCELONA IN THE END.

20 MAY

DID YOU KNOW THAT THERE IS A PLACE THAT IS LOCATED IN TWO COUNTRIES AT THE SAME TIME? THIS IS THE PHEASANTRY ISLAND, WHICH IS SHARED BY FRANCE AND SPAIN DUE TO A 350 AN AGREEMENT THAT IS MORE THAN 30 YEARS OLD: SPAIN HAS TO LOOK AFTER IT FROM FEBRUARY TO JULY, AND FRANCE FROM AUGUST TO JANUARY.

21 MAY

DESPITE WHAT EVERYONE BELIEVES, THE FIRST CROISSANT WAS NOT FRENCH... IT WAS ACTUALLY AUSTRIAN, CREATED 190 YEARS AGO.

22
MAY

THE OLDEST LIGHTHOUSE IN THE WORLD IS IN SPAIN, SPECIFICALLY IN GALICIA. IT'S THE HERCULES TOWER, WHICH IS STILL WORKING AFTER 2,000 YEARS. CAN YOU IMAGINE HOW MANY INCREDIBLE STORIES IT COULD TELL US ABOUT ALL THE PIRATE SHIPS IT HAS SEEN PASSING BY?

23
MAY

DID YOU KNOW THAT THERE ARE MORE THAN 7000 LANGUAGES SPOKEN IN THE WORLD? THE COUNTRY WITH THE MOST LANGUAGES IS PAPUA NEW GUINEA, WHERE 838 DIFFERENT LANGUAGES ARE SPOKEN.

**24 MAY**

IF OUR BODY WAS A COMPANY, IT WOULD BE BOSSED BY OUR BRAIN. THIS BIG BOSS IS IN CHARGE OF OUR WHOLE ORGANISM AND IT IS ALSO THE ONLY ORGAN THAT DOES NOT FEEL PAIN.

**25 MAY**

DID YOU KNOW THAT ALMOST 40,000 DIFFERENT BACTERIA LIVE IN YOUR MOUTH? YOU MAY THINK THIS IS IMPRESSIVE, BUT THEY ARE THERE TO HELP YOU. BUT YOU HAVE TO TAKE CARE OF THEM TOO, SO REMEMBER TO BRUSH YOUR TEETH WELL AFTER EATING!

**26 MAY**

HAVE YOU EVER NOTICED THAT WHEN YOU'RE EMBARRASSED ABOUT SOMETHING, YOU TURN RED AS A TOMATO? BELIEVE IT OR NOT, YOUR STOMACH DOES TOO!

**27**
MAY

DID YOU KNOW THAT EVERY YEAR YOU LOSE 4 KILOS (8.8 POUNDS) OF SKIN? LIKE A SNAKE, WE ALSO CHANGE OUR DEAD SKIN FOR NEW SKIN... EVEN UP TO 8 TIMES A YEAR!

**28**
MAY

HAIR GROWS VERY FAST, BUT DID YOU KNOW THAT IT GROWS EVEN FASTER IN SUMMER? THIS IS BECAUSE THE HEAT CAUSES VASODILATION, A PROCESS THAT MAKES YOUR HAIR GROW FASTER.

**29**
MAY

OUR BLOOD CELLS ARE GREAT ATHLETES: THEY ARE ABLE TO RUN THROUGH OUR WHOLE BODY IN JUST 60 SECONDS.

30 MAY

CAMELS ARE REAL WATER CONTAINERS! THEY CAN DRINK 106 LITRES (23 GALLONS) OF WATER IN ONE GO, WHICH IS THE SAME AS MORE THAN ONE HUNDRED 1-LITRE BOTTLES! AFTER ALL, THEY NEED A LOT OF WATER TO LAST THE 10 DAYS IN THE DESERT WITHOUT A DROP OF WATER.

31 MAY

. DO YOU THINK THERE IS ANYTHING HOTTER THAN THE SUN? THE ANSWER IS YES, AND THAT IS THE CENTRE OF THE PLANET WE LIVE ON. THE EARTH'S INNER CORE REACHES A TEMPERATURE OF 6,000 DEGREES CENTIGRADE (10,832 FAHRENHEIT), HOTTER THAN THE SURFACE OF THE SUN.

01 JUNE

HAVE YOU EVER IMAGINED A TREE PLANTED UPSIDE DOWN? WELL, THE CLOSEST THING WOULD BE THE BAOBAB, ALSO KNOWN AS THE MONKEY BREAD OR UPSIDE-DOWN TREE. APART FROM ITS UNUSUAL SHAPE, THIS TREE HOLDS UP TO 1,000 LITRES OF WATER DURING TIMES OF DROUGHT, WHICH IS WHY IT IS ALSO KNOWN AS THE CAMEL TREE.

**02** JUNE

CACTUSES ARE LIKE CAMELS, NOT BECAUSE THEY DRINK MANY LITRES OF WATER, BUT BECAUSE OF THEIR GREAT CAPACITY TO STORE IT. THEIR THICK WAXY COATING AND THORNS MEAN THAT THEY CAN HOLD THE WATER IN HUMIDITY TO BE ABLE TO ABSORB IT SLOWLY.

**03** JUNE

WHEN YOU TOUCH YOUR FOREHEAD YOU WON'T NOTICE THAT IT IS VERY HOT UNLESS YOU HAVE A FEVER. BUT THE HEAT YOUR BODY GIVES OFF IS MUCH MORE THAN YOU IMAGINE: IN JUST 30 MINUTES, YOU COULD BOIL ALMOST HALF A LITRE OF WATER.

**04** JUNE

IF I STARTED TALKING ABOUT A CAMEL, YOU WOULD PROBABLY THINK OF ONE WALKING SLOWLY THROUGH THE DESERT. BUT DID YOU KNOW THAT THEY CAN ALSO SWIM IN DEEP WATER?

**05**
JUNE

IF WE COULD REMEMBER OUR DREAMS, WE COULD WRITE A BOOK AND TELL MANY STORIES. WE HAVE BETWEEN 4 AND 6 DIFFERENT DREAMS EVERY NIGHT WHILE WE ARE ASLEEP.

**06**
JUNE

YOU WOULDN'T WANT TO BE A WORKER ANT... AFTER LOOKING FOR FOOD, BUILDING AN ANTHILL, AND RAISING THE FUTURE QUEEN ANTS, THESE ANTS ONLY SLEEP 4 HOURS A DAY AND HAVE SHORT DREAMS THAT LAST A FEW MINUTES. IT WOULD BE BETTER TO BE THE QUEEN THAT SLEEPS DOUBLE THAT TIME.

**07**
JUNE

WOULD YOU BE ABLE TO SLEEP STANDING UP? ALTHOUGH THEY'RE INCREDIBLY TALL, GIRAFFES CAN DO THIS. GIRAFFES ONLY SLEEP FOR 2 OR 3 HOURS A DAY, AND NOT ALL IN ONE GO, HAVING DREAMS FOR 5 AND 7 MINUTES AT THE MOST. THEY ALSO SLEEP LYING ON THEIR LEGS OR FORMING AN ARCH WITH THEIR LONG NECKS.

08
JUNE

DID YOU KNOW THAT WHILE WE SLEEP WE ARE ABLE TO HOLD OUR BREATH? YOU MAY NOT REALISE IT, BUT DURING OUR SLEEP WE MAY STOP BREATHING FOR SEVERAL MINUTES.

09
JUNE

CAN YOU IMAGINE SPENDING MORE THAN HALF YOUR LIFE SLEEPING? HOW BORING! WELL, THAT’ S WHAT CATS DO FOR MORE THAN 70% OF THEIR LIVES. THE REST OF THE TIME THEY WASH THEMSELVES AND SPEND ABOUT 10,950 HOURS PURRING.

10
JUNE

IF YOU SAW A GROUP OF OTTERS SLEEPING IN THE WATER, YOU WOULD NOTICE THAT THEY WOULD BE HOLDING HANDS. IT SEEMS LIKE SUCH A CUTE GESTURE TO US, BUT THEY DO THIS FOR SURVIVAL SO THEY DON’T LOSE THEIR WAY OR GET LOST. OTTERS ALSO HAVE A VERY SPECIAL POCKET IN THEIR FUR WHERE THEY CAN KEEP THEIR FAVOURITE ROCK.

11 JUNE

IF YOU ARE TOO FLIRTY, PEOPLE WILL TELL YOU THAT “YOU LOOK IN THE MIRROR TOO MUCH.” UNLESS YOU ARE IN SERBIA, WHERE PEOPLE SAY YOU “TOUCH THE CLOUDS WITH YOUR NOSE”. THEY USE THE EXPRESSION, “NOSOM PARA OBLAKE”, WHICH IN THEIR LANGUAGE REFERS TO A VERY VAIN PERSON.

12 JUNE

DID YOU KNOW THAT THE “NAVEL OF THE MOON” IS NOT ON THE MOON? ACTUALLY, WHEN WE TALK ABOUT MEXICO, THE COUNTRY’S NAME EXPRESSES THE MEANING: “METXI” (MOON), “XICTLI “ (NAVEL), AND “CO” (PLACE). THE AZTEC PEOPLE ESTABLISHED IT ON THE LAKE OF TEXCOCO, WHICH MEANS THE “LAKE OF THE MOON”.

13 JUNE

WHEN WE ARE VERY SAD, IT IS AS IF WE HAVE A COLD IN OUR SOULS. THIS IS HOW JAPANESE PEOPLE DESCRIBE IT WITH THE WORD “KOKORO NO KAZE”, MEANING SOMEONE WHO IS DEPRESSED.

14
JUNE

COULD YOU WRITE FROM RIGHT TO LEFT WITHOUT USING A SINGLE VOWEL? PROBABLY NOT, BUT THE ARABS CAN. THEY HAVE A LANGUAGE MADE UP OF 3 VOWELS AND 22 CONSONANTS, AND A CONSONANT-ONLY SCRIPT THAT THE READER FILLS IN WITH THE MISSING VOWEL.

15
JUNE

DID YOU KNOW THAT WHEN YOU TAKE A "PHOTOGRAPH" YOU ARE LITERALLY WRITING WITH LIGHT? THIS IS BECAUSE THE MEANING OF THE WORD COMES FROM THE GREEK, WHERE "FOTO" MEANS LIGHT AND "GRAFIA" MEANS WRITING.

16
JUNE

DO YOU KNOW WHAT CITY HAS THE LONGEST NAME IN THE WORLD? BANGKOK (THAILAND)! YES, THE NAME LOOKS SHORT, BUT THIS IS ONLY WHAT PEOPLE FROM ABROAD KNOW THE CITY AS. ITS REAL NAME IS: "KRUNG THEP MAHANAKHON AMON RATTANAKOSIN MAHINTHARA AYUTHAYA MAHADILOK PHOP NOPPHARAT RATCHATHANI BURIROM UDOMRATCHANIWET MAHASATHAN AMON PIMAN AWATAN SATHIT SAKKATHATTIYA WITSANUKAM PRASIT". IF YOU SAY "KRUNG THEP MAHANAKHON", THE THAIS WILL UNDERSTAND YOU.

17
JUNE

WHICH FAMOUS SUPERHERO CAN JUMP FROM ONE BUILDING TO ANOTHER IN JUST ONE JUMP? THE ANSWER IS SUPERMAN, WHO DIDN'T ACTUALLY FLY AND ONLY HAD THE POWER TO JUMP VERY HIGH. IT WAS FROM THE 1940S THAT THEY MADE HIM MUCH MORE POWERFUL AND GAVE HIM THE ABILITY TO FLY LIKE A BULLET AT FULL SPEED.

18
JUNE

DID YOU KNOW THAT ELEPHANTS CAN'T JUMP? IF THEY DID, THEY COULDN'T SUPPORT THEIR WEIGHT AND WOULD END UP BREAKING THEIR HUGE LEGS.

19
JUNE

THE SURFACE OF THE MOON IS LIKE A GIANT TRAMPOLINE: IF YOU JUMPED ON IT, YOU WOULD BE ABLE TO GO ALMOST 3 METRES (9.8 FEET) HIGH.

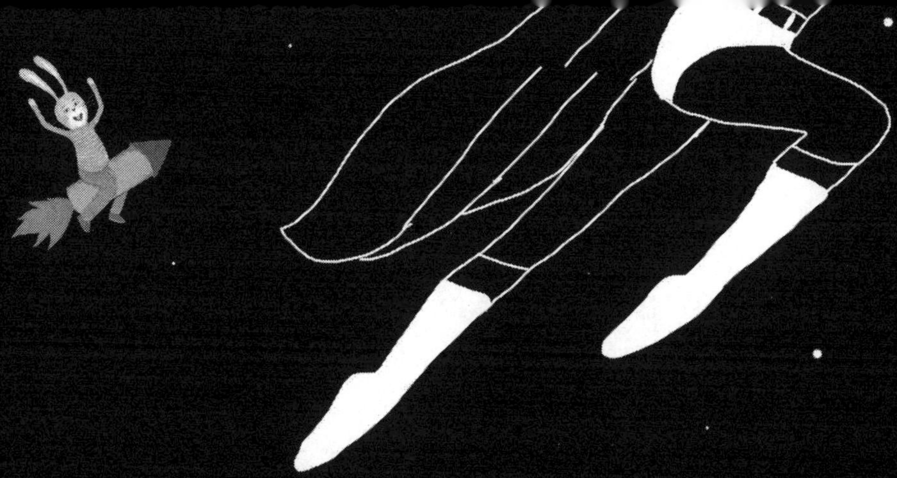

**20** JUNE

THERE'S NO DOUBT THAT KANGAROOS ARE THE BEST AT JUMPING, BUT DID YOU KNOW THAT THEY CAN'T JUMP BACKWARDS?

**21** JUNE

CAN YOU IMAGINE A COUNTRY WITH MORE KANGAROOS THAN PEOPLE? THIS IS THE CASE IN AUSTRALIA, WHERE THERE ARE MORE THAN 2 KANGAROOS PER PERSON.

**22** JUNE

MANY ANIMALS HAVE 4 LEGS, BUT ONLY ONE HAS 4 KNEES. THIS IS THE ELEPHANT, THE ONLY ANIMAL THAT ALSO MANAGES TO KNEEL WITH ITS FRONT LEGS, BUT INSTEAD OF ELBOWS, IT HAS TWO MORE KNEES.

23
JUNE

IF YOU EVER WANT TO TRAVEL BY HITCHHIKING, THE BEST COUNTRY IS DEFINITELY CUBA! IF A GOVERNMENT CAR DRIVES PAST WITH A FREE SEAT, THEY HAVE TO PICK YOU UP.

24
JUNE

CHINA HAS AT LEAST 67 MILLION EMPTY HOUSES. THERE ARE SO MANY THAT THEY COULD BE FILLED WITH THE ENTIRE POPULATION OF THE UNITED KINGDOM.

25
JUNE

DID YOU KNOW THAT IN THE UNITED KINGDOM YOU CAN FIND SOME VERY INTERESTING MUSEUMS? ONE OF THEM IS THE MARBLES MUSEUM. IT IS A VERY UNIQUE MUSEUM FULL OF HISTORY, WHERE YOU CAN HAVE A MARBLE RACE ON THE BIGGEST MARBLE TRACK IN THE UNITED KINGDOM.

**26** JUNE

"THE POOREST PRESIDENT IN THE WORLD" WAS PEPE MUJICA, FORMER PRESIDENT OF URUGUAY. HE WAS CALLED THIS BECAUSE HE ONLY KEPT 10 PERCENT OF HIS SALARY AND DONATED THE REST TO THOSE IN NEED: HE LIVED IN A SIMPLE HOUSE AND TRAVELLED IN AN OLD CAR.

**27** JUNE

1 IN 5 PEOPLE IN THE WORLD LIVE IN CHINA, AS IT IS THE MOST POPULATED COUNTRY IN THE WORLD WITH 18.25 PERCENT OF THE WORLD'S POPULATION.

**28** JUNE

IF YOU LIKE WALKING ON A FLAT SURFACE AND ARE AFRAID OF HEIGHTS, I RECOMMEND A TRIP TO BOLIVIA, THE FLATTEST COUNTRY IN THE WORLD. THERE ARE ALSO BEAUTIFUL LANDSCAPES SUCH AS THE UYUNI SALT FLAT, THE LONGEST SALT DESERT IN THE WORLD WITH 10,500 SQUARE METRES (2.6 ACRES) OF SALT, AND ONE OF THE MOST IMPORTANT RESERVES OF LITHIUM.

29 JUNE

WOULD YOU LIKE TO CARRY A BIKE? NOT JUST ANY BIKE, BUT THE LIGHTEST ONE. IT WEIGHS ONLY 2.7 KILOS (6 POUNDS), WHICH IS MUCH LESS THAN A CAT.

30 JUNE

DID YOU KNOW THAT FOOTBALL WAS INVENTED BY THE CHINESE OVER 2,000 YEARS AGO? AND IT WASN'T ALWAYS ABOUT SCORING GOALS, IT WAS ALSO ABOUT KEEPING THE BALL IN THE AIR FOR AS LONG AS POSSIBLE.

01 JULY

COULD YOU IMAGINE AN OLIMPIC GAMES WHERE THERE WERE MUSICIANS, PAINTERS AND SCULPTORS AS WELL AS ATHLETES? WELL, THAT'S HOW IT WAS BETWEEN 1912 AND 1948, FOR ALMOST 40 YEARS WHEN ART WAS ALSO PART OF THIS GREAT COMPETITION.

**02** JULY

DO YOU KNOW THE SYMBOL OF THE OLYMPICS? DID YOU KNOW THAT ITS 5 CIRCLES REPRESENT THE 5 CONTINENTS AND ITS COLOURS REPRESENT THE FLAGS OF THE FIRST COUNTRIES THAT COMPETED IN THE OLYMPICS? THIS WAS THE IDEA OF PIERRE FREDY DE COUBERTIN, WHO WAS THE FOUNDER OF THE OLYMPIC GAMES, AND A FRENCH TEACHER AND HISTORIAN.

**03** JULY

THE OLYMPICS ARE A SYMBOL OF PEACE AND SOLIDARITY. IN ANCIENT GREECE, THEY STOPPED ALL WARS BECAUSE THEY WERE NOT ALLOWED TO TAKE PLACE DURING THE OLYMPICS.

**04** JULY

CAN YOU IMAGINE HAVING TO SING AN ANTHEM WITH 158 VERSES? THE NATIONAL ANTHEM OF GREECE IS THE LONGEST IN THE WORLD. ALTHOUGH LUCKILY FOR THE GREEKS, THIS WAS THE ORIGINAL SONG FROM WHICH ONLY 2 VERSES ARE SUNG TODAY.

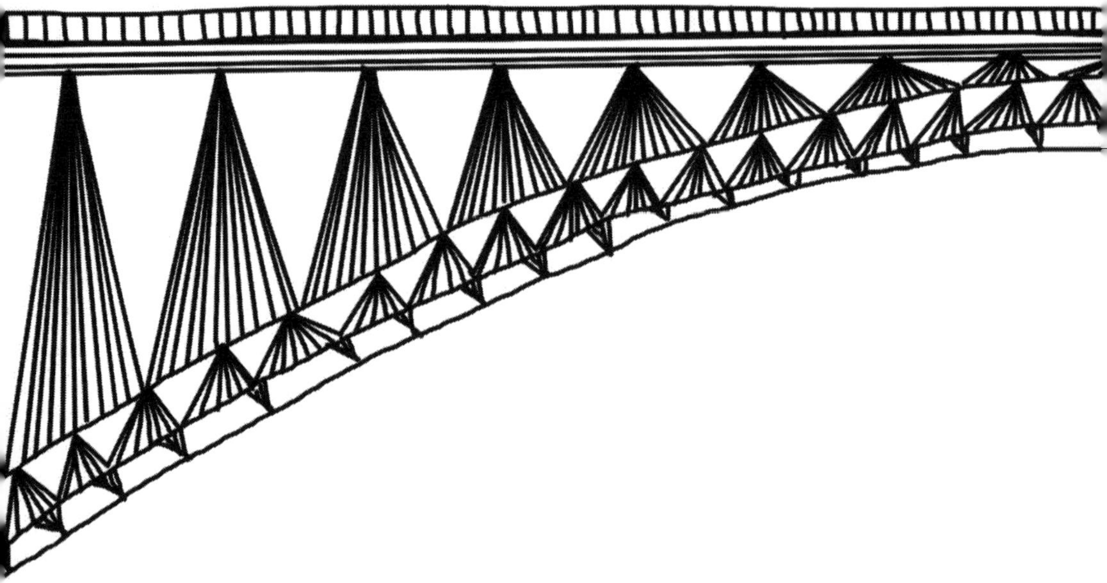

05 JULY

WOULD YOU DARE TO CROSS A BRIDGE MADE FROM THE LIVING ROOTS OF A TREE? IN INDONESIA, THERE IS A BRIDGE BUILT LIKE THIS AND IT IS 25 METRES (82 FEET) LONG, CONNECTING TWO VILLAGES ON THE BATANG BAYANG RIVER. IT TOOK AS MANY AS 26 YEARS TO BUILD.

06 JULY

SOME BRIDGES ARE LONGER THAN OTHERS, WHILE OTHERS ARE WIDER THAN THEY ARE LONG. THIS IS THE CASE OF THE O'CONNELL BRIDGE, THE ONLY BRIDGE IN EUROPE THAT IS 5.5 METRES (18 FEET) WIDER THAN IT IS LONG.

07 JULY

THE WORLD'S LARGEST LIVING ORGANISM IS NEITHER A PLANT NOR AN ANIMAL... IT IS A HUGE MUSHROOM CALLED ARMILLARIA OSTAYAE THAT IS 2,400 YEARS OLD AND AS BIG AS... 1,665 FOOTBALL PITCHES! IT HAS SPREAD THROUGHOUT THE FOREST, KILLING HUNDREDS OF TREES TO TAKE UP A TOTAL AREA OF NEARLY 4 SQUARED MILES (10 SQUARED KILOMETRES). NO WONDER IT IS KNOWN AS "THE OREGON MONSTER".

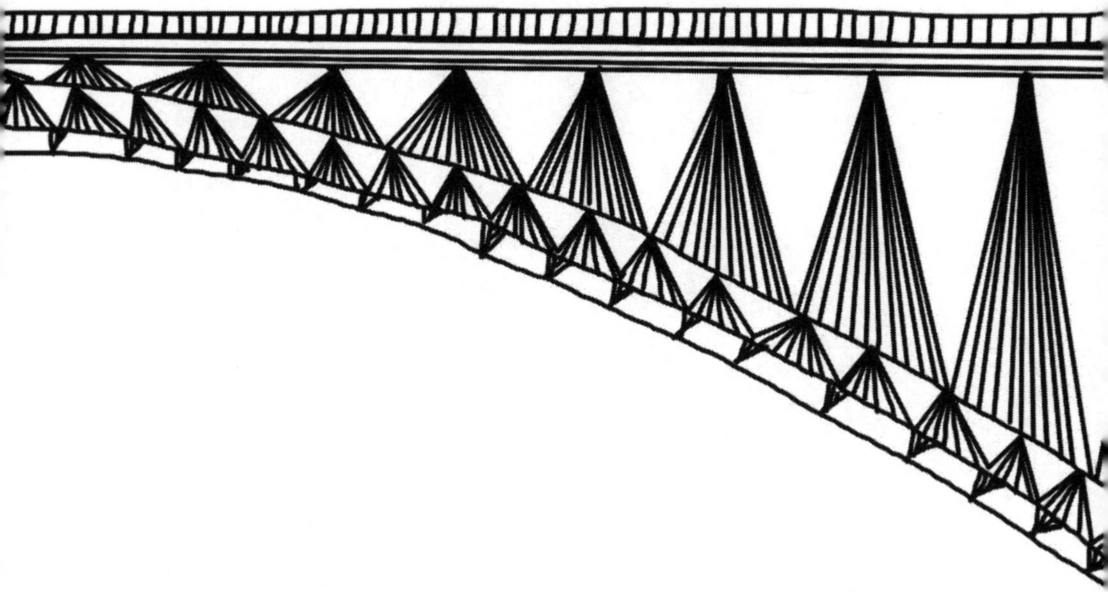

08 JULY

THE GREAT WALL OF CHINA IS NOT JUST A GREAT WALL. WITH ITS 13,170 MILES IN LENGTH, IT IS THE LONGEST MAN-MADE STRUCTURE IN THE WORLD. FOR YOU TO HAVE AN IDEA, THIS IS THE DISTANCE IN A STRAIGHT LINE FROM BARCELONA TO TOKYO, THERE AND BACK!

09 JULY

CAN YOU IMAGINE SWINGING 2,600 METRES (8,530 FEET) ABOVE THE GROUND? IF YOU WANT TO, YOU CAN DO THIS IN ECUADOR ON WHAT THEY CALL “THE SWING AT THE END OF THE WORLD”. IT IS BUILT ON THE EDGE OF A CLIFF AND ALLOWS YOU TO SWING OVER AN AMAZING CLIFF.

10 JULY

ONCE UPON A TIME THERE WAS A CAVE AS TALL AS A 28-STOREY BUILDING AND SO BIG THAT YOU COULD PARK AS MANY AS 10 PLANES INSIDE IT. IT WAS DISCOVERED IN 1981 IN THE GUNUNG NATIONAL PARK IN SARAWAK (MALAYSIA), MAKING IT THE LARGEST UNDERGROUND CAVE IN THE WORLD WITH A HEIGHT OF 70 METRES (230 FEET), A LENGTH OF 700 METRES (2,300 FEET), AND A WIDTH OF 400 METRES (1,312 FEET).

11 JULY

YOU DON'T HAVE TO STICK OUT YOUR TONGUE IF YOU WANT TO MOVE IT. YOU ACTUALLY MAKE THOUSANDS OF MOVEMENTS WITH IT WITHOUT REALISING: IT EXPANDS, CONTRACTS, FLATTENS, AND CONTRACTS AGAIN... AND SO ON ALL DAY LONG WITHOUT STOPPING.

12 JULY

IF YOU ARE ABLE TO TOUCH YOUR NOSE WITH YOUR TONGUE, THEN MANY PEOPLE WILL BE JEALOUS OF YOU... AND EVEN CROCODILES. CROCODILES CAN'T STICK OUT THEIR TONGUES, WHICH CAN ONLY MOVE A FEW CENTIMETRES, NOT BECAUSE THEY ARE UNSKILFUL, BUT BECAUSE THEY HAVE THEIR TONGUE ATTACHED TO THE ROOF OF THEIR MOUTH.

13 JULY

IF A CAT'S TONGUE SURPRISES YOU WITH ITS ROUGH TEXTURE, IMAGINE WHAT A TIGER'S TONGUE IS LIKE, WHICH IS ABLE TO RIP THE PAINT OFF THE WALL IN A SINGLE LICK.

**14** JULY

SOME PEOPLE USE LARGE SCISSORS TO TEAR LEAVES AND BRANCHES FROM TREES, AND OTHERS USE THEIR OWN TONGUE, LIKE THE GIRAFFE. GIRAFFES USE THEIR TONGUES TO EAT, WHICH CAN BE AS LONG AS 50 CENTIMETRES (20 INCHES).

**15** JULY

IF YOU ARE ABLE TO DISTINGUISH BETWEEN SWEET AND SALTY, IT IS NOT BECAUSE YOU ARE A GREAT CHEF, BUT BECAUSE OF THE TASTE BUDS ON YOUR TONGUE, WHERE THERE ARE AS MANY AS 3,000 OF THEM! NOT ALL PEOPLE HAVE THE SAME NUMBER, SO SOMETIMES WHAT SEEMS VERY TASTY TO YOU MIGHT NOT BE TO SOMEONE ELSE. TASTE BUDS ARE RESPONSIBLE FOR TELLING THE DIFFERENCE BETWEEN FLAVOURS AND CHOOSING YOUR FAVOURITE DISHES, BUT THEY ARE ALSO THE REASON WHY YOU DON'T LIKE CERTAIN TYPES OF FOODS AS MUCH.

**16** JULY

IF YOU RUB SLICED ONION OR GARLIC ON THE SOLES OF YOUR FEET, HALF AN HOUR LATER… YOU WILL FEEL THE TASTE IN YOUR MOUTH! DO YOU HAVE THE NERVE TO TRY IT?

## 17 JULY

NOT ONLY DO MOTHERS TAKE CARE OF THEIR CHILDREN, BUT BABIES TAKE CARE OF THEIR MOTHERS TOO. ACTUALLY, YOU DID THIS WHILE EVERYONE WAS WAITING FOR YOU TO BE BORN. WHEN YOU WERE JUST A FETUS, BY A PROCESS CALLED UTERINE MICROCHIMERISM, YOU COULD HEAL YOUR MUM BY SENDING YOUR STEM CELLS TO HER DAMAGED ORGANS.

## 18 JULY

DID YOU KNOW THAT THE LINES ON YOUR HANDS WERE THERE BEFORE YOU WERE BORN? THEY WERE FORMED WHEN YOU WERE ONLY 3 MONTHS OLD AND BECAUSE OF THEM, YOU CAN BEND YOUR HANDS WITHOUT STRETCHING YOUR SKIN.

## 19 JULY

THE EMBRACE OF A MOTHER AND HER NEWBORN BABY IS NOT ONLY A WONDERFUL ACT OF LOVE BUT ALSO OF SURVIVAL. THE BABY'S SMELL SENDS SIGNALS TO THE MOTHER'S IMMUNE SYSTEM, SO THE ANTIBODIES IN THE MOTHER'S MILK WILL FEED THE BABY AND PROTECT THEM FROM ILLNESSES.

**20**
JULY

A BABY'S BODY IS VERY SMALL, BUT DID YOU KNOW THAT IT HAS UP TO 100 MORE BONES THAN AN ADULT'S BODY? BECAUSE THE BIGGER WE GET, THE FEWER BONES WE HAVE, AS THEY JOIN TOGETHER AS WE GROW. THAT'S WHY WE ARE BORN WITH 300 BONES AND WHEN WE GROW UP WE HAVE 206.

**21**
JULY

SEAHORSES ARE VERY FAITHFUL ANIMALS: THE MOTHER AND FATHER ARE TOGETHER ALL THEIR LIVES, THAT'S WHY WE CALL THEM MONOGAMOUS. BELIEVE IT OR NOT, THE FATHER CARRIES THE BABY INSIDE HIM BEFORE THE BABY IS BORN, AND NOT THE MOTHER.

**22**
JULY

IT IS IMPOSSIBLE TO SWALLOW AND BREATHE AT THE SAME TIME... UNLESS YOU ARE A BABY. UNTIL THEY ARE 6 OR 7 MONTHS OLD, BABIES CAN DO THIS THANKS TO THEIR LARYNX: SINCE IT IS HIGHER, IT LEAVES MORE SPACE BETWEEN THE TRACHEA, THE TUBE THROUGH WHICH AIR PASSES, AND THE OESOPHAGUS, THE TUBE THROUGH WHICH FOOD PASSES. THIS IS WHY THEY CAN DRINK THEIR MOTHER'S MILK WITHOUT CHOKING.

23
JULY

DID YOU KNOW THAT VATICAN HAS ONE OF THE GREATEST WEALTH IN THE WORLD? SECOND ONLY TO THE UNITED STATES, THEIR FORTUNE IS COUNTLESS: WITH THE MONEY THEY HAVE, THEY COULD END WORLD POVERTY AND NOT JUST ONCE, BUT TWICE.

24
JULY

TWO OLYMPIC SWIMMING POOLS FULL OF GOLD MAY SEEM LIKE A HUGE FORTUNE. BUT DID YOU KNOW THAT THIS IS ALL THE GOLD THAT HAS EVER BEEN MINED? APPROXIMATELY 165,000 TONNES (363 MILLION POUNDS) OF A PRECIOUS METAL IS A REALLY LOW AMOUNT. TO GIVE YOU AN IDEA, WE PRODUCE THE SAME AMOUNT OF STEEL, IN JUST ONE HOUR!

25
JULY

REMEMBERING THE NAME PABLO PICASSO MAY SEEM EASY. BUT DID YOU KNOW THAT HIS REAL NAME WAS PABLO DIEGO JOSÉ FRANCISCO DE PAULA JUAN NEPOMUCENO MARÍA DE LOS REMEDIOS CIPRIANO DE LA SANTÍSIMA TRINIDAD RUIZ Y PICASSO? DO YOU THINK YOU CAN REMEMBER THAT?

26

JULY

DO YOU KNOW LEONARDO DA VINCI, THE FAMOUS ARTIST WHO PAINTED THE "MONA LISA"? IN ADDITION TO BEING A PAINTER, AN ENGINEER, AND AN ARCHITECT, THIS GREAT GENIUS WAS ALSO A VERY CURIOUS PERSON WHO MADE GREAT INVENTIONS. HE WAS ABLE TO DRAW A BICYCLE, AN AIRPLANE, AND A HELICOPTER, MANY YEARS BEFORE THEY WERE ACTUALLY INVENTED.

27

JULY

HOW MANY PHOTOS HAVE YOU TAKEN TODAY? IF YOU ADDED UP ALL THE PHOTOS THAT WE CAN TAKE IN JUST 2 MINUTES, THAT WOULD BE MORE THAN ALL THE PHOTOS TAKEN IN 100 YEARS IN THE 19TH CENTURY.

28

JULY

IF YOUR TUMMY HURTS, POUR MORE KETCHUP ON IT! THIS MAY SEEM CRAZY TO YOU, BUT NOT TO DR JOHN COOK BENNETT. IN THE 1830S, HE SOLD IT AS A MEDICINE EVEN IN THE FORM OF PILLS FOR DIARRHOEA AND INDIGESTION. HE THOUGHT TOMATOES COULD CURE THESE DISEASES.

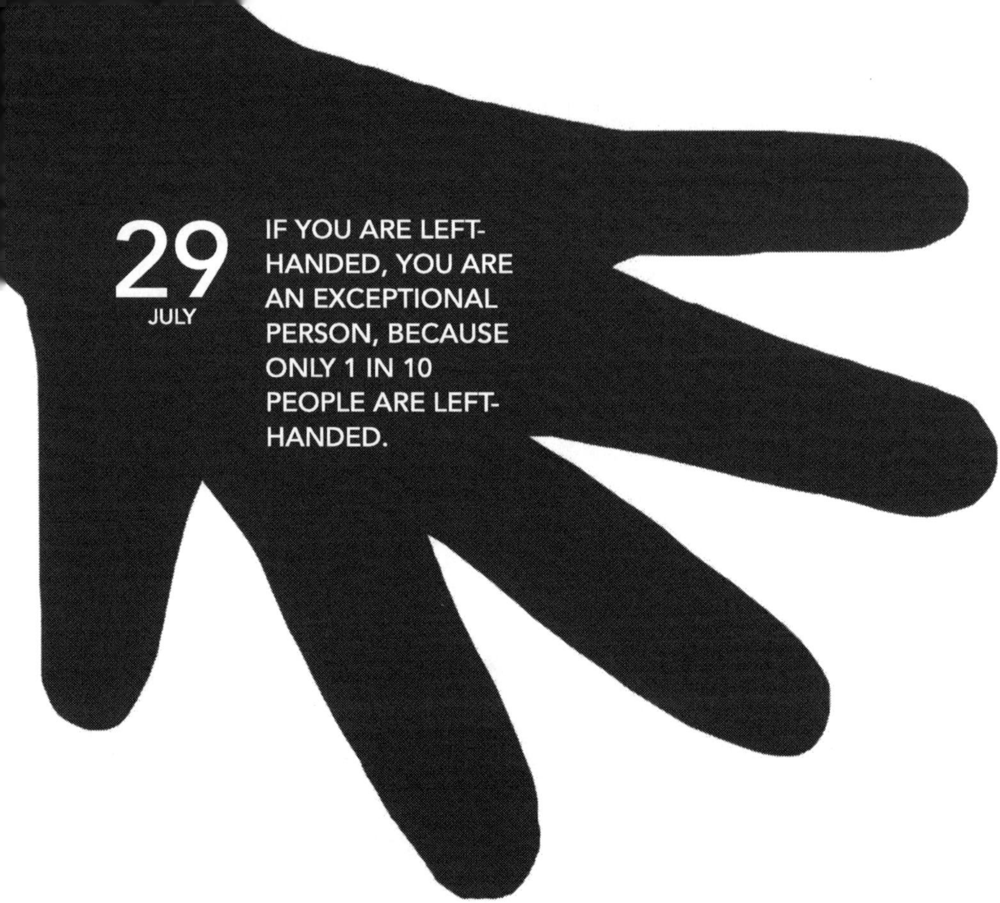

**29** JULY

IF YOU ARE LEFT-HANDED, YOU ARE AN EXCEPTIONAL PERSON, BECAUSE ONLY 1 IN 10 PEOPLE ARE LEFT-HANDED.

**30** JULY

HAVE YOU NOTICED THAT YOU ALMOST ALWAYS CHEW YOUR FOOD WITH THE RIGHT SIDE OF YOUR MOUTH? WELL, THAT IS IF YOU ARE A RIGHT-HANDED PERSON BECAUSE IF YOU ARE LEFT-HANDED YOU WILL USE THE LEFT SIDE OF YOUR MOUTH.

**31** JULY

CAN YOU IMAGINE IF YOUR SHOES WERE EXACTLY THE SAME SHAPE FOR BOTH FEET? HOW UNCOMFORTABLE! WELL, THAT'S HOW PEOPLE HAD TO WALK UNTIL THE 19TH CENTURY WHEN IN PHILADELPHIA THEY MADE THE FIRST SHOES THAT SEPARATED LEFT AND RIGHT FEET.

**01**
**AUGUST**

YOUR BIRTHDAY IS A VERY SPECIAL DAY. SO SPECIAL THAT YOU COULD CELEBRATE IT WITH APPROXIMATELY 9 MILLION OTHER PEOPLE WHO ALSO SHARE THE SAME BIRTHDAY.

**02**
**AUGUST**

TO FIND OUT IF YOUR DOG IS LEFT- OR RIGHT-HANDED, HIDE SOME FOOD IN YOUR HAND AND SEE WHICH PAW HE/SHE TRIES TO TAKE IT WITH. THAT'S RIGHT, THEY ALSO HAVE THIS ABILITY, AS DO OTHER ANIMALS SUCH AS CATS, GORILLAS, AND CRABS.

**03**
**AUGUST**

ON THE DAY YOU CELEBRATE YOUR 31ST BIRTHDAY YOU CAN ALSO CELEBRATE ONE BILLION SECONDS OF LIFE.

**04**
AUGUST

THERE'S NO NEED TO BE IN A HURRY, JUST TELL THAT TO THE GARDEN SNAIL. THEY ARE THE SLOWEST ANIMALS IN THE WORLD, TAKING UP TO 1 HOUR TO TRAVEL JUST 50 METRES

**05**
AUGUST

CHEETAHS CAN BOAST ABOUT BEING THE FASTEST ANIMAL IN THE WORLD, BUT ONLY ON LAND. THEY CAN OUTRUN A CAR ON A MOTORWAY AT A SPEED OF 120 KILOMETRES PER HOUR.

**06**
AUGUST

THE PEREGRINE FALCON IS NOT ONLY THE FASTEST ANIMAL IN THE SKY BUT ALSO IN THE WHOLE WORLD. THIS BIRD CAN FLY AS FAST AS A HIGH-SPEED TRAIN AT 300 KILOMETRES PER HOUR.

**07**
AUGUST

IF YOU LIKE DINOSAURS, YOU PROBABLY KNOW THE FAMOUS T-REX. BUT DID YOU KNOW THAT IT WAS THE SLOWEST OF ALL THE DINOSAURS THAT EXISTED? THEY WERE AS SLOW AS A BICYCLE AND SLOWER THAN A GREAT ATHLETE, RUNNING AT A SPEED OF ONLY 18 MILES PER HOUR.

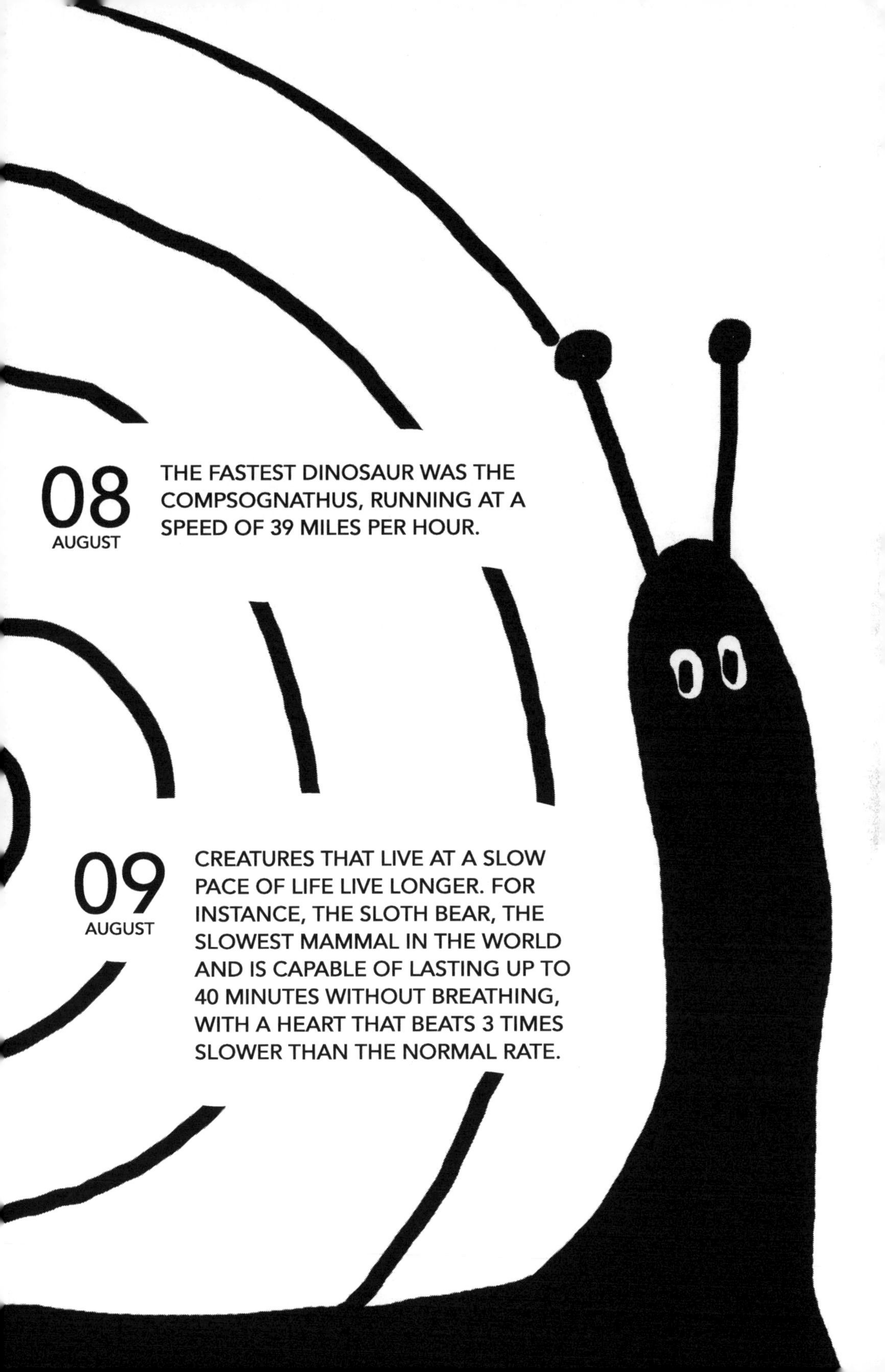

08
AUGUST

THE FASTEST DINOSAUR WAS THE COMPSOGNATHUS, RUNNING AT A SPEED OF 39 MILES PER HOUR.

09
AUGUST

CREATURES THAT LIVE AT A SLOW PACE OF LIFE LIVE LONGER. FOR INSTANCE, THE SLOTH BEAR, THE SLOWEST MAMMAL IN THE WORLD AND IS CAPABLE OF LASTING UP TO 40 MINUTES WITHOUT BREATHING, WITH A HEART THAT BEATS 3 TIMES SLOWER THAN THE NORMAL RATE.

**10**
AUGUST

COULD YOU IMAGINE LIVING IN A PLACE WHERE THERE WERE NO REPTILES AND AMPHIBIANS? THEN YOU WOULD BE IN ANTARCTICA, THE ONLY CONTINENT ON THE PLANET WHERE THESE SPECIES OF ANIMALS DO NOT EXIST.

**11**
AUGUST

THE GLOBE IS ROUND, BUT IT IS DIVIDED INTO HALVES THAT ARE VERY UNEQUAL. ONLY 12 OUT OF EVERY 100 PEOPLE LIVE IN THE SOUTHERN HEMISPHERE, AS OPPOSED TO THE NORTHERN HALF WHERE 88 PERCENT OF THE WORLD'S POPULATION IS LOCATED.

**12**
AUGUST

AFRICA IS THE ONLY CONTINENT THAT CAN CLAIM TO BE IN 4 HEMISPHERES AT THE SAME TIME: NORTH, SOUTH, EAST, AND WEST.

**13**
AUGUST

COULD YOU BE IN EUROPE AND ASIA AT THE SAME TIME? AS IMPOSSIBLE AS IT MAY SEEM TO YOU, YOU CAN DO THIS IF YOU EVER TRAVEL TO ISTANBUL. THIS IS THE ONLY CITY IN THE WORLD THAT IS LOCATED IN TWO CONTINENTS, CONNECTED BY THE BOSPHORUS STRAIT.

**14**
AUGUST

DID YOU KNOW THAT THERE ARE AS MANY PEOPLE IN THE URBAN AREA OF TOKYO AS THERE ARE IN ALL OF CANADA? THE CAPITAL OF JAPAN IS THE MOST POPULATED CITY IN THE WORLD WITH 37,340,000 PEOPLE.

**15**
AUGUST

THE PEOPLE OF SINGAPORE MUST FEEL VERY SPECIAL TO LIVE IN THE ONLY PLACE IN THE WORLD THAT IS A CITY, AN ISLAND, AND A COUNTRY ALL AT THE SAME TIME.

16
AUGUST

DID YOU KNOW THAT YOUR TEETH ARE ALMOST AS HARD AS A ROCK? THE ENAMEL THAT COVERS THEM IS ACTUALLY THE HARDEST SUBSTANCE IN YOUR BODY.

17
AUGUST

COULD YOU IMAGINE HAVING MORE THAN 9,000 TEETH IN YOUR MOUTH? THE CATFISH HAS THIS NUMBER OF TEETH, MAKING IT THE ANIMAL WITH THE MOST TEETH IN THE WORLD AND IT LIVES IN ASIA AND AMERICA.

18
AUGUST

THE GREY WHALE IS THE WORLD CHAMPION OF MIGRATION: TO RETURN HOME, EACH YEAR IT MAKES A ROUND TRIP OF 14,384 MILES FROM THE ARCTIC TO MEXICO, WHICH IS MORE THAN THE DISTANCE FROM THE NORTH POLE TO THE SOUTH POLE.

**19**
AUGUST

CAN YOU IMAGINE SAYING SOMETHING IN MADRID AND BEING HEARD IN LONDON? WHALES CAN COMMUNICATE AT THIS DISTANCE IN THE SEA.

**20**
AUGUST

THE LION'S ROAR CAN BE HEARD FROM AS FAR AS 5 MILES AWAY!

**21**
AUGUST

IF YOU SEE A WHALE OR DOLPHIN WITH ONE EYE OPEN IT IS NOT BECAUSE THEY ARE WINKING AT YOU, THEY MAY ALSO BE SLEEPING. THIS HAPPENS BECAUSE HALF OF THEIR BRAIN IS AWAKE WHILE THEY SLEEP.

22
AUGUST

THE EARTHWORM HAS NO EYES, LEGS, OR BONES, BUT IT DOES HAVE 10 HEARTS SPREAD OUT ON THE LENGTH OF ITS BODY.

23
AUGUST

SOME SAY THAT OCTOPUSES ARE ALIENS, AND NO WONDER WHY! THIS UNIQUE ANIMAL HAS 9 BRAINS, 8 ARMS, AND 3 HEARTS.

24
AUGUST

YOU ARE ALL HEART! NOT YOU, BUT THE BLUE WHALE, WHICH IS THE ANIMAL WITH THE LARGEST HEART IN THE WORLD. IT CAN BE AS TALL AS A PERSON AND WEIGH AS MUCH AS A SMALL CAR, REACHING UP TO 680KG (1,500 POUNDS).

**25**
AUGUST

DID YOU KNOW THAT BABIES BREATHE FASTER? THEIR HEART BEATS 70 TO 190 TIMES A MINUTE WHEN THEY ARE NEWBORNS, AS OPPOSED TO 60 TO 80 TIMES A MINUTE FOR ADULTS.

**26**
AUGUST

IF YOU HOLD A LARGE FIST AND CLENCH IT, YOU CAN SEE THE SIZE OF YOUR HEART.

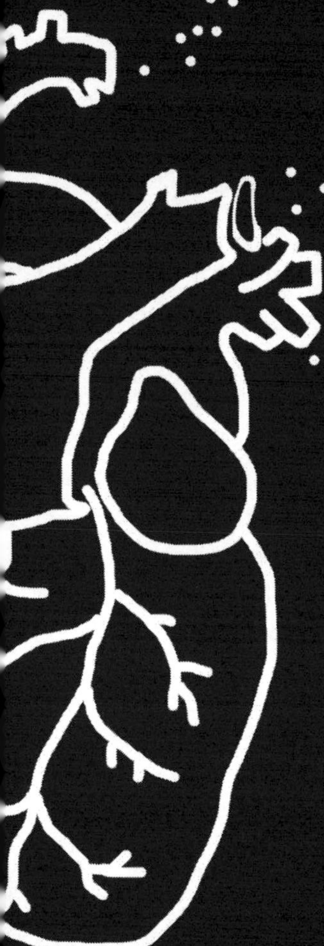

**27**
AUGUST

IF YOU PUT YOUR HAND ON YOUR CHEST AND FEEL YOUR HEART BEATING, YOU COULD COUNT UP TO 100,000 BEATS IN A DAY.

**28**
AUGUST

THE RINGS OF SATURN ARE NOT REALLY RINGS AT ALL. THEY LOOK LIKE THAT FROM A DISTANCE, BUT IF WE WERE TO GET CLOSER WE WOULD SEE THAT THEY ARE A BUNCH OF ROCKS, DUST, AND ICE PARTICLES THAT DIDN'T COME TOGETHER TO FORM A SATELLITE. SOME ARE AS SMALL AS A GRAIN OF SAND AND SOME ARE THE SIZE OF SKYSCRAPERS.

**29**
AUGUST

HOW COOL IT WOULD BE TO LIVE ON URANUS, WHERE IT IS SUMMER FOR 21 YEARS! THIS IS THE LENGTH OF THE 4 SEASONS ON THIS PLANET, BECAUSE OF THE HUGE TILT OF ITS AXIS. HOWEVER, WE WOULD HAVE TO SPEND 21 YEARS IN CONSTANT LIGHT, AND ANOTHER 21 YEARS IN WINTER AND TOTAL DARKNESS.

**30**
AUGUST

IF YOU WENT DOWN A TUNNEL THROUGH THE CENTRE OF THE EARTH, IT WOULD TAKE YOU 42 MINUTES AND 12 SECONDS TO GO ALL THE WAY THROUGH.

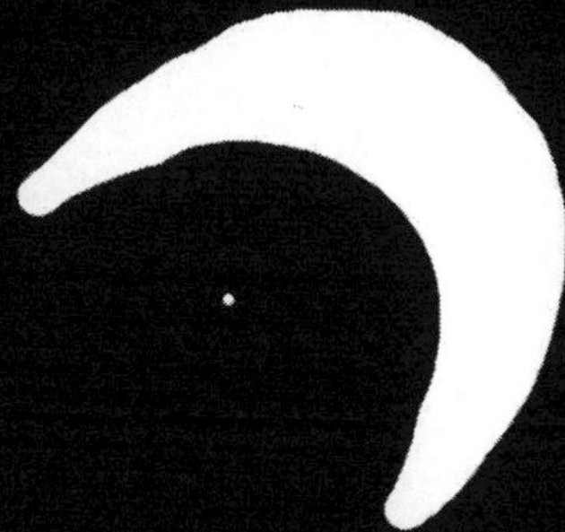

31
AUGUST

CAN YOU IMAGINE HOW LONG IT WOULD TAKE YOU TO REACH THE SURFACE OF THE SUN? WELL, SUNLIGHT ONLY TAKES 8 MINUTES AND 17 SECONDS TO REACH THE SURFACE OF THE EARTH.

01
SEPTEMBER

THE DAYS ON VENUS ARE VERY LONG! VENUS TAKES A LONG TIME TO SPIN AROUND, WHICH MEANS THAT 1 SINGLE DAY ON VENUS IS... 246 DAYS ON EARTH!

02
SEPTEMBER

IT WOULD TAKE YOU ALMOST A YEAR TO WALK AROUND THE PLANET EARTH, ON A CIRCUMFERENCE THAT IS ABOUT 25,000 MILES LONG. WALKING AT 3 MILES PER HOUR, IT WOULD TAKE YOU 330 DAYS.

## 03 SEPTEMBER

DID YOU KNOW THAT YOU ARE ABLE TO MOVE A CAR FOR 20 MILES? WELL, MAYBE NOT YOU, BUT YOUR HEART COULD, GIVEN THE POWER THAT THIS GREAT MUSCLE CAN GENERATE IN A SINGLE DAY.

## 04 SEPTEMBER

YOU'VE PROBABLY WONDERED WHAT YOUR LITTLE FINGER IS FOR... DID YOU KNOW THAT IF YOU DIDN'T HAVE IT, YOUR HAND WOULD LOSE HALF ITS STRENGTH? IN FACT, EVERY PART OF OUR BODY HAS A VERY IMPORTANT FUNCTION, NO MATTER HOW USELESS OR UNIMPORTANT WE MAY THINK THEY ARE.

## 05 SEPTEMBER

DID YOU KNOW THAT THE SPIDER IS CAPABLE OF MAKING A MATERIAL STRONGER THAN STEEL? THE SILK IT PRODUCES WITH ITS WEB CAN WITHSTAND A WEIGHT OF 0.5 GRAMS WITHOUT BREAKING, MORE THAN A STEEL THREAD THAT WOULD BREAK AT HALF THE WEIGHT.

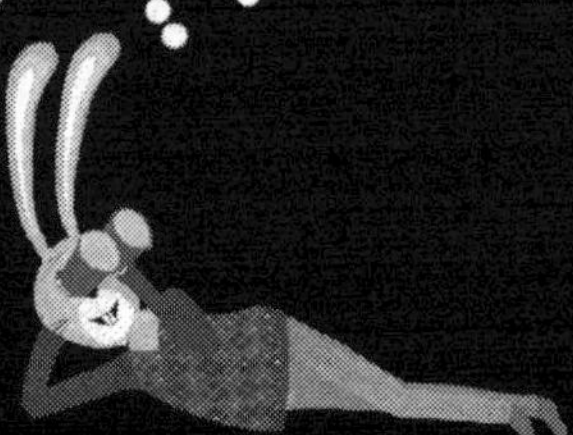

**06 SEPTEMBER**

WOULD YOU BE ABLE TO CARRY 60 CHILDREN LIKE YOURSELF ON A HORSE? THIS IS WHAT ANTS DO, AS THEY CAN CARRY UP TO 60 TIMES THEIR OWN WEIGHT.

**07 SEPTEMBER**

MANY BELIEVE THAT OUR STRONGEST MUSCLE IS OUR TONGUE. WE SHOULDN'T TAKE ANYTHING AWAY FROM THIS SUPER MUSCLE THAT WE MOVE SO MUCH DURING THE DAY, BUT IF WE HAVE TO CHOOSE THE TOUGHEST AND STRONGEST OF ALL, IT IS... OUR BUM! IT TAKES A LOT OF STRENGTH TO STAND UP STRAIGHT, ALLOWING US TO PLAY AND RUN FOR SO MANY HOURS A DAY.

**08 SEPTEMBER**

THE HEAVIEST OF ALL SPIDERS AND ONE OF THE LARGEST IS THE GOLIATH TARANTULA, WHICH WEIGHS AS MUCH AS AN APPLE AND IS 28 CENTIMETRES (11 INCHES) LONG. LIKE OTHER SPIDERS, GOLIATH TARANTULAS FEED ON INSECTS, BUT THEY ALSO FEED ON RATS AND LIZARDS. IN ORDER TO CATCH THEIR PREY, THEY FALL ON THEM AND INJECT THEIR VENOM BY BITING THEM WITH THEIR POWERFUL JAWS.

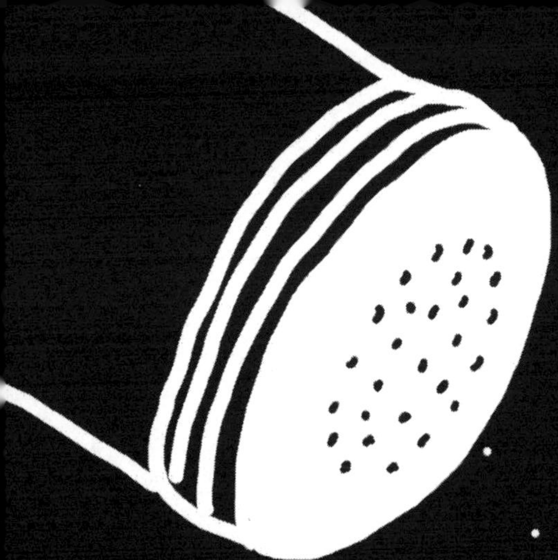

09 SEPTEMBER

CAN YOU IMAGINE LIVING UNDER THE SEA? WELL, INCREDIBLE AS IT MAY SEEM, THAT'S WHAT THEY DO IN SOME CITIES AROUND THE WORLD THAT ARE BELOW SEA LEVEL: TWO OF THEM ARE AMSTERDAM IN THE NETHERLANDS, AT 1 METRE (3.2 FEET) BELOW THE SEA, AND BAKU IN AZERBAIJAN AT -28 METRES (-92 FEET).

10 SEPTEMBER

ALL FISH FEAR THE DEAD SEA BECAUSE ONLY BACTERIA AND ALGAE CAN SURVIVE THERE. THE DEAD SEA IS 6 TO 7 TIMES SALTIER THAN THE OTHER OCEANS IN THE WORLD, SO IF ANY AQUATIC ANIMAL GOES THERE BY ACCIDENT, THEY WILL DIE COVERED IN SALT CRYSTALS. NO WONDER THE DEAD SEA HAS ITS NAME.

11 SEPTEMBER

IF YOUR EYES ITCH WHEN YOU CRY, IT'S NOT BECAUSE YOUR TEARS WANT TO ANNOY YOU. THE REASON IS THAT YOUR TEARS ARE SALTY LIKE SEAWATER, BUT THE SEA HAS 4 TIMES THE AMOUNT OF SALT.

12
SEPTEMBER

DID YOU KNOW THAT THE PACIFIC OCEAN IS LESS SALTY THAN THE ATLANTIC OCEAN? THIS IS BECAUSE THE WATER FROM THE PACIFIC EVAPORATES AND IS TURNED INTO CLOUDS, WHICH THEN FIND A NATURAL BARRIER IN THE ROCKY MOUNTAINS OF NORTH AMERICA AND THE ANDES MOUNTAIN RANGE IN SOUTH AMERICA. INSTEAD OF GOING TO THE ATLANTIC, IT BECOMES RAIN THAT FALLS ON THE MOUNTAINS AND GOES BACK TO THE OCEAN, MAKING IT LESS SALTY.

13
SEPTEMBER

ONCE UPON A TIME THERE WAS AN OCEAN WITH WATER SO PEACEFUL THAT IT WAS CALLED THE PACIFIC OCEAN. THIS IS HOW IT WAS FOR THE PORTUGUESE NAVIGATOR FERNANDO DE MAGELLAN, WHO TRAVELLED THROUGH STORMY WATERS IN NOVEMBER 1520. WHEN HE PASSED OVER WHAT WE KNOW TODAY AS THE STRAIT OF MAGELLAN, HE FOUND CALM ("PEACEFUL") WATER WITH GOOD WIND FOR NAVIGATION.

14
SEPTEMBER

DID YOU KNOW THAT THERE IS MUCH MORE WATER THAN LAND ON PLANET EARTH? ACTUALLY, THREE-QUARTERS OF THE EARTH'S SURFACE IS COVERED BY WATER, MAINLY FROM THE OCEANS. YOU MIGHT ALSO BE SURPRISED IN TERMS OF THE AMOUNT OF SPACE TAKEN: WATER COVERS 361 MILLION OUT OF THE 510 MILLION SQUARE KILOMETRES OF THE EARTH'S SURFACE.

**15** SEPTEMBER

WHAT DOES ONE ANT SAY TO ANOTHER? LONG LIVE THE QUEEN! THIS IS BECAUSE QUEEN ANTS LIVE UP TO 30 YEARS, WHILE WORKER ANTS ONLY LIVE UP TO 3 YEARS.

**16** SEPTEMBER

DID YOU KNOW THAT IT TAKES 1,440,000 FLOWERS TO PRODUCE 1 KILO OF HONEY? AS WELL AS THE WORK OF 200 WORKER BEES, WHICH TRAVEL AS FAR AS 40 KILOMETRES DURING THEIR SHORT 50-DAY LIFESPAN. SO BE CAREFUL NOT TO DROP THE HONEY, OR YOU WILL HAVE RUINED THEIR HARD WORK!

**17** SEPTEMBER

DID YOU KNOW THAT COCKROACHES CAN LIVE UP TO A WEEK WITHOUT A HEAD? THIS IS BECAUSE THEY HAVE THEIR BRAINS IN ANOTHER PART OF THEIR BODY.

**18** SEPTEMBER

IF YOU SWEAT A LOT AND YOUR BLOOD TYPE IS 0, BEWARE OF MOSQUITOES AS YOU WILL BE ONE OF THEIR FAVOURITES! THAT'S WHY PEOPLE DON'T GET BITTEN AS MUCH AS OTHERS.

**19** SEPTEMBER

IF YOU MANAGED TO COLLECT 30,000 QUADRILLION FIREFLIES, YOU WOULD HAVE THE SAME AMOUNT OF LIGHT THAT THE SUN PRODUCES AS THESE INSECTS ARE MAGICALLY ILLUMINATED.

**20** SEPTEMBER

LIKE THE LIVING DEAD COMING OUT OF THEIR GRAVES AND REAPPEARING AFTER 17 YEARS UNDERGROUND... NO, I'M NOT TALKING ABOUT ZOMBIES! CICADAS ARE INSECTS THAT SPEND ALL THESE YEARS EATING ROOTS UNDERGROUND, ALL BEFORE THEY SEE THE SUNLIGHT FOR THE LAST 2 TO 4 WEEKS OF THEIR LIVES.

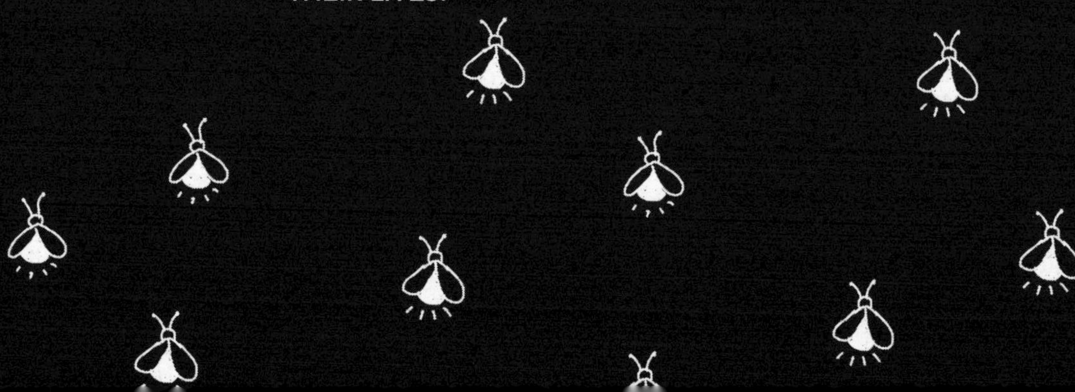

21
SEPTEMBER

DID YOU KNOW THAT OWLS ARE THE ONLY BIRDS THAT CAN SEE THE COLOUR BLUE?

22
SEPTEMBER

NO MATTER HOW MUCH YOU MAY BE TOLD: JUST REMEMBER WHAT I TELL YOU! YOUR MEMORY IS ALWAYS MORE LIKELY TO REMEMBER WHAT YOU'VE SEEN THAN WHAT YOU'VE HEARD.

23
SEPTEMBER

YOU NEED TO HAVE VERY GOOD EYES TO BE AN EAGLE! DUE TO HAVING EYESIGHT THAT IS 4 TO 8 TIMES MORE POWERFUL THAN THAT OF A HUMAN, AN EAGLE IS ABLE TO SEE A TINY ANT FROM THE 10TH FLOOR OF A BUILDING!

**24**
SEPTEMBER

IF YOU SEE A PIG LYING PEACEFULLY IN THE SUN, IT IS NOT BECAUSE IT WANTS TO GET A TAN, IT IS MORE LIKELY TO BE TAKING THE OPPORTUNITY TO LOOK AT THE SKY, WHICH IT CAN NEVER SEE WHEN STANDING ON ITS FEET.

**25**
SEPTEMBER

IF YOU GO INTO THE FOREST REMEMBER TO COME BACK BEFORE IT GETS DARK... UNLESS YOU ARE A TIGER, WHICH HAS NIGHT VISION UP TO 6 TIMES MORE POWERFUL THAN OURS.

**26**
SEPTEMBER

IS IT POSSIBLE TO BE THE BIGGEST BIRD IN THE WORLD WITH A BRAIN AS SMALL AS A WALNUT? WELL YES, AND THIS BIRD IS THE OSTRICH, WHICH HAS EYES THE SAME SIZE AS A SAUCER AND BIGGER THAN THE SIZE OF ITS BRAIN.

**27** SEPTEMBER

CAN YOU IMAGINE BEING ABLE TO TRAVEL IN A BALLOON EVERY DAY OF THE YEAR? CAPPADOCIA HOSTS THE HOT AIR BALLOON FESTIVAL, A COLOURFUL SPECTACLE THAT FILLS THE TURKISH SKY, WHERE YOU CAN GO UP IN THE HOT AIR BALLOON AT ANY TIME (DEPENDING ON THE WEATHER, OF COURSE!).

**28** SEPTEMBER

YOU'LL HAVE TO PRACTICE A LOT TO MAKE THE WORLD'S BIGGEST BUBBLEGUM BUBBLE. AN AMERICAN WOMAN DID IT IN 1994, BREAKING THE GUINNESS RECORD BY BLOWING A BUBBLE 58 CENTIMETRES, A SIZE BIGGER THAN A BICYCLE WHEEL!

**29** SEPTEMBER

IF YOU LIKE SHEEP, NEW ZEALAND IS THE PLACE FOR YOU. IT IS THE COUNTRY WITH THE MOST SHEEP IN THE WORLD WITH APPROXIMATELY 7 SHEEP FOR EVERY PERSON. IMAGINE THE COLLECTION OF WOOLLEN SCARVES YOU COULD HAVE THERE!

**30**
SEPTEMBER

50 YEARS AGO THEY INVENTED THE FIRST MOBILE PHONE, 30 YEARS AGO NOT MANY PEOPLE HAD ONE, AND NOW THERE ARE MORE MOBILE PHONES THAN PEOPLE IN THE WORLD.

**01**
OCTOBER

IF YOU TRAVEL TO ROME, YOU DON'T NEED TO WAIT FOR YOUR BIRTHDAY TO BE ABLE TO MAKE A WISH. PEOPLE IN ROME TOSS COINS INTO THE TREVI FOUNTAIN IN THE HOPE THAT THEIR DREAMS COME TRUE. THERE ARE SO MANY COINS THAT UP TO 4,000 EUROS COULD BE COLLECTED EVERY DAY!

**02**
OCTOBER

ITALY IS AN AMAZING COUNTRY, BUT NOT ONLY BECAUSE OF ITS DELICIOUS FOOD. IT HAS TWO OTHER COUNTRIES INSIDE IT THAT ARE INDEPENDENT STATES: SAN MARINO AND VATICAN CITY.

03
OCTOBER

T WOULD TAKE MANY MILES TO GO ALL THE WAY AROUND THE WORLD. BUT DID YOU KNOW THAT YOU WOULD BE ABLE TO DO THIS IF YOU STRETCHED EVERY VEIN IN YOUR BODY? AND NOT JUST GOING THE EARTH AROUND ONCE... BUT TWO AND A HALF TIMES!

04
OCTOBER

HOW MANY PEOPLE ARE THERE IN THE WORLD? SO MANY! BUT DID YOU KNOW THAT THERE ARE MORE BACTERIAL CELLS IN YOUR BODY? THERE ARE APPROXIMATELY... 10 TRILLION BACTERIA LIVING INSIDE YOUR BODY!

05
OCTOBER

IF WE THINK ABOUT THE AMOUNT OF WATER ON OUR PLANET, IT MAY SEEM LIKE A HUGE AMOUNT. IN FACT, THERE ARE 1,234 TRILLION LITRES OF WATER ON EARTH, WHICH IS A LOT, BUT YOU MIGHT BE SURPRISED TO KNOW THAT ONLY 2.5 PERCENT OF THAT WATER IS FRESH AND JUST 0.3 PERCENT IS DRINKABLE. THIS AMOUNT OF WATER IS ALSO BEING REDUCED BECAUSE OF POLLUTION.

**06** OCTOBER

HAVE YOU EVER SEEN A SHOOTING STAR? EVEN THOUGH WE MAY THINK THEY ARE BIG, A SHOOTING STAR IS NOTHING MORE THAN A STONE OR AS IT IS OFFICIALLY CALLED -A METEOR, WHICH IS THE SIZE OF A PEBBLE.

**07** OCTOBER

A PLACE WHERE IT HARDLY EVER RAINS TENDS TO BE A VERY DRY REGION, BUT THIS IS NOT THE CASE IN ANTARCTICA: THE PLACE WITH THE LEAST RAINFALL ON THE PLANET HAS PLENTY OF WATER, MAKING UP 80 PERCENT OF ALL WATER IN THE WORLD.

**08** OCTOBER

THE UNIVERSE AND ITS SOLAR SYSTEM ARE INFINITE! IF THE EARTH SEEMS BIG TO YOU, IMAGINE THE SIZE OF URANUS, WHICH COULD FIT 63 PLANETS OF OUR SIZE. BUT THE AWARD FOR THE BIGGEST PLANET IN THE SOLAR SYSTEM GOES TO THE GIANT JUPITER, WHICH COULD HOLD AS MANY AS... 1,300 EARTHS!

**09**
OCTOBER

SOME PEOPLE SAY THAT LIFE IS ROSY AND OTHERS SEE IT ALL IN BLACK. BUT IN FACT, OUR EYES CAN SEE 10 MILLION DIFFERENT COLOURS! SO, WHAT COLOUR DO YOU SEE LIFE IN?

**10**
OCTOBER

DESPITE WHAT WE THINK ABOUT BULLS, THEY DO NOT ANGRY BECAUSE OF THE COLOUR RED. THEY CAN'T EVEN SEE THE COLOUR RED BECAUSE THEY ARE APPARENTLY COLOUR BLIND AND IT'S ACTUALLY MOVEMENT THAT REALLY ANNOYS THEM.

**11**
OCTOBER

ALTHOUGH YOU MAY FIND IT HARD TO BELIEVE, NOT ALL OF US HAVE RED BLOOD. CRICKETS, FOR EXAMPLE, HAVE WHITE BLOOD, JUST LIKE OTHER INSECTS. THIS IS BECAUSE THEY DON'T NEED HAEMOGLOBIN, WHICH IS A PROTEIN THAT CARRIES OXYGEN IN OUR BODIES AND MAKES OUR BLOOD RED.

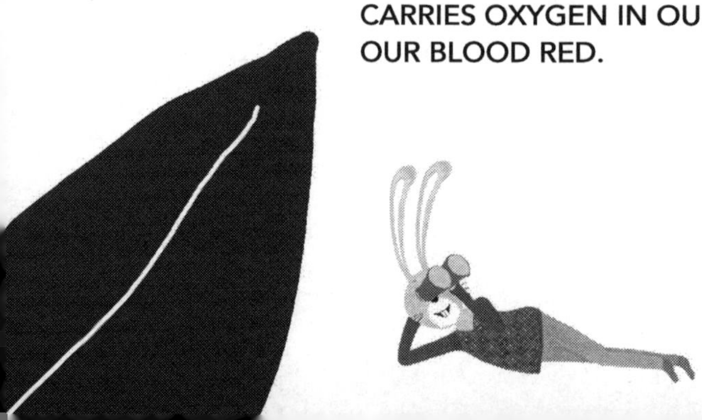

**12**
OCTOBER

IF HEDGEHOGS SEE LIFE IN YELLOW, IT'S NOT BECAUSE THEY'RE FEELING CHEERFUL OR ARE VERY INTELLIGENT... IT IS BECAUSE IT IS THE ONLY COLOUR THEY SEE AND ALSO IN A FEW SHADES.

**13**
OCTOBER

NO ONE IS AS GOOD AT COPYING AS THE THAUMOCTOPUS MIMICUS, AN OCTOPUS THAT CAN CHANGE COLOUR UP TO 15 TIMES TO MATCH THAT OF OTHER SEA CREATURES.

**14**
OCTOBER

WHAT COLOUR WOULD YOU FEEL WHEN YOU ARE VERY HAPPY? WHAT COLOUR WOULD YOU FEEL WHEN YOU ARE SAD OR ANGRY? ALTHOUGH WE CAN'T CHANGE COLOURS, CHAMELEONS CAN CHANGE THE COLOUR OF THEIR SKIN DEPENDING ON HOW THEY FEEL.

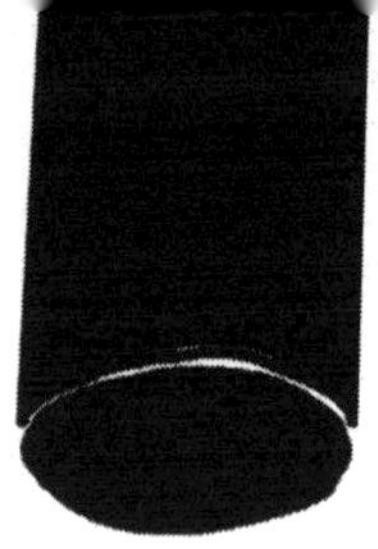

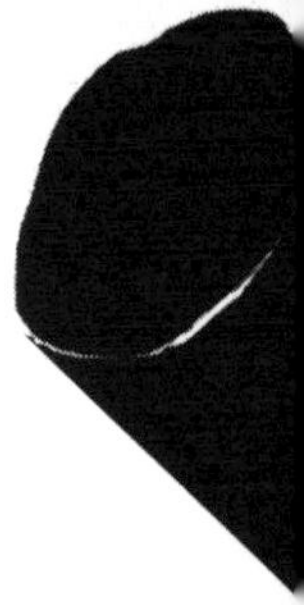

15 OCTOBER

CAN YOU IMAGINE ENTERING A LARGE CAVE FULL OF HUGE BLOCKS OF CRYSTAL? THIS IS THE CAVE OF CRYSTALS, WHICH IS IN MEXICO AND IS ABOUT 300 METRES BELOW THE GROUND. ITS GYPSUM CRYSTAL PILLARS ARE ALMOST AS TALL AS A 4-STOREY BUILDING, ONE OF THE LARGEST NATURAL CRYSTALS EVER KNOWN.

16 OCTOBER

IN THE UNITED STATES, THERE IS A PLACE WHERE THE ROCKS MOVE BY THEMSELVES, INCLUDING THE HEAVIEST ONES THAT WEIGH 200KG (440 POUNDS)! THIS IS THE DEATH VALLEY, THE MOST UNIQUE, MAGICAL, AND CRAZY LANDSCAPE IN THE WORLD. IT WAS A MYSTERY FOR A LONG TIME UNTIL PEOPLE DISCOVERED THAT WHEN IT RAINS, THE LAKE WHERE THE ROCKS ARE LOCATED BECOMES COVERED WITH A LAYER OF ICE, WHICH MELTS WHEN THE SUN RISES, CAUSING THE ROCKS TO BE PUSHED AROUND EASILY.

17 OCTOBER

HOW NICE IT WOULD BE IF WE DIDN'T HAVE TO WRAP UP IN BIG JACKETS AND HEAVY COATS. ONE EXAMPLE IS IN NAURU AND THE MARSHALL ISLANDS, TWO PLACES IN OCEANIA THAT WOULD NEVER NEED THEM AS THE TEMPERATURE HAS NEVER DROPPED BELOW 20 DEGREES CELSIUS (68 DEGREE FAHRENHEIT).

**18** OCTOBER

IF YOU EVER TRAVEL TO LISBON, REMEMBER THAT UNDER YOUR FEET THERE ARE HIDDEN TUNNELS, BRIDGES, CORRIDORS, AND CHAMBERS... THAT ARE OVER 2,000 YEARS OLD! IN FACT, LISBON IS ONE OF THE OLDEST CITIES IN THE WORLD AND WAS FOUNDED MORE THAN 3,000 YEARS AGO. IT IS THE SECOND OLDEST EUROPEAN CAPITAL AFTER ATHENS, BUT IT'S AHEAD OF ROME.

**19** OCTOBER

DID YOU KNOW THAT IN AUSTRALIA THERE IS A BUBBLEGUM PINK LAKE? ALTHOUGH IT DOESN'T LOOK REAL... IT ACTUALLY IS. LAKE HILLIER IS LOCATED IN THE ARCHIPELAGO OF RECHERCHE, WHICH IS A TRUE GIFT OF NATURE, WHERE BACTERIA AND THE HIGH SALT CONTENT CREATE THIS WONDERFUL COLOUR. AND IF YOU DARE TO SWIM IN IT, YOU'LL FLOAT LIKE A CORK!

**20** OCTOBER

IF YOU OPEN A BOTTLE OF WINE, IT IS VERY LIKELY THAT ITS CORK HAS TRAVELLED ALL THE WAY FROM PORTUGAL. THIS COUNTRY IS THE LARGEST PRODUCER OF CORK, MAKING 160,000 TONNES (353 MILLION POUNDS) OF CORK A YEAR, MORE THAN HALF OF WHAT IS PRODUCED IN THE WHOLE WORLD, WHERE 5 TO 6 MILLION CORKS ARE MADE THERE EVERY DAY.

**21** OCTOBER

IF YOU'RE EVER TOLD "YOU WILL GET STRUCK LIGHTNING!" DON'T TAKE IT TOO SERIOUSLY... UNLESS YOU'RE IN THE DEMOCRATIC REPUBLIC OF CONGO. THIS COUNTRY HAS THE HIGHEST NUMBER OF LIGHTNING STRIKES IN THE WORLD IN ONE YEAR, WITH ALMOST 70 STRIKES PER SQUARE KILOMETRE.

**22** OCTOBER

IF I TOLD YOU THAT 100 LIGHTNING STRIKES HIT THE EARTH EVERY SECOND, YOU WOULD PROBABLY NOT BE VERY SURPRISED. BUT WHAT IF I ALSO TOLD YOU THAT EACH LIGHTNING STRIKE HAS A POWER OF UP TO 30 MILLION VOLTS AND A TEMPERATURE FIVE TIMES HOTTER THAN THE SURFACE OF THE SUN? NOW, DOES THIS SURPRISE YOU?

**23** OCTOBER

CAN YOU IMAGINE BEING ABLE TO BATHE IN THE WATER OF A RAINBOW? THE CLOSEST YOUCOULD GET TO SOMETHING LIKE THIS IS THE GRAND PRISMATIC SPRING IN THE YELLOWSTONE NATIONAL PARK, UNITED STATES. THE MINERALS AND BACTERIA MAKE THE WATER BLUE, GREEN, ORANGE, YELLOW, RED... HARDLY ANY COLOURS ARE MISSING! BUT IT IS A SHAME THAT THE AVERAGE TEMPERATURE IS 70 DEGREES CELSIUS (158 DEGREES FAHRENHEIT).

**24**
OCTOBER

THERE ARE ROADS WHERE YOU COULD (ALMOST) FRY AN EGG... BUT THERE ARE ALSO RIVERS WHERE YOU COULD BOIL ONE! SUCH AS THE RIVER THAT IS HIDDEN IN THE PERUVIAN AMAZON, WHERE THE WATER IS BOILING AND STEAMY.

**25**
OCTOBER

DID YOU KNOW THAT RAINBOWS ARE NOT ACTUALLY SHAPED LIKE ARCHES? THEY ARE EVEN MORE BEAUTIFUL THAN HOW WE SEE THEM, HAVING A CIRCULAR SHAPE THAT HAS NO START AND NO END. BUT, WE WILL HAVE TO SETTLE WITH THE FACT THAT WE CAN ONLY SEE ONE PART OF IT AS THE HALF IS CUT OFF BY THE HORIZON.

**26**
OCTOBER

IF YOU WANT TO SEE THE RAREST PLANTS, BUGS, AND ANIMALS IN THE WORLD, YOU SHOULD TRAVEL TO BRAZIL, COLOMBIA, OR INDONESIA. MORE SPECIES LIVE IN THESE COUNTRIES THAN ALL THE OTHER COUNTRIES ON THE PLANET COMBINED, WITH BRAZIL HAVING THE MOST. HOWEVER, COLOMBIA HAS THE MOST SPECIES PER SQUARE KILOMETRE AND THE HIGHEST NUMBER OF ENDEMIC SPECIES, WHICH ARE THOSE THAT ARE NOT FOUND ANYWHERE ELSE.

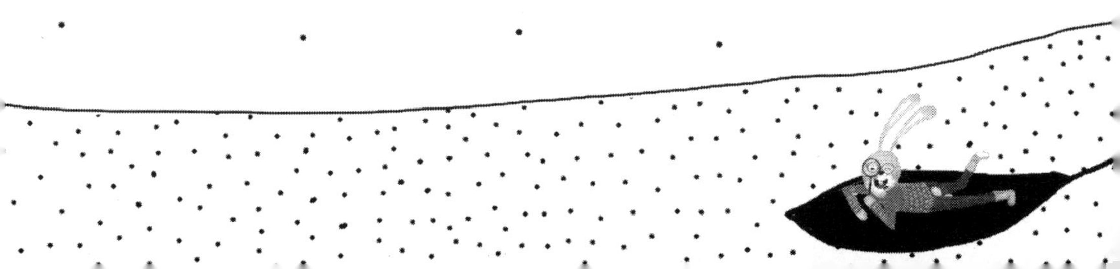

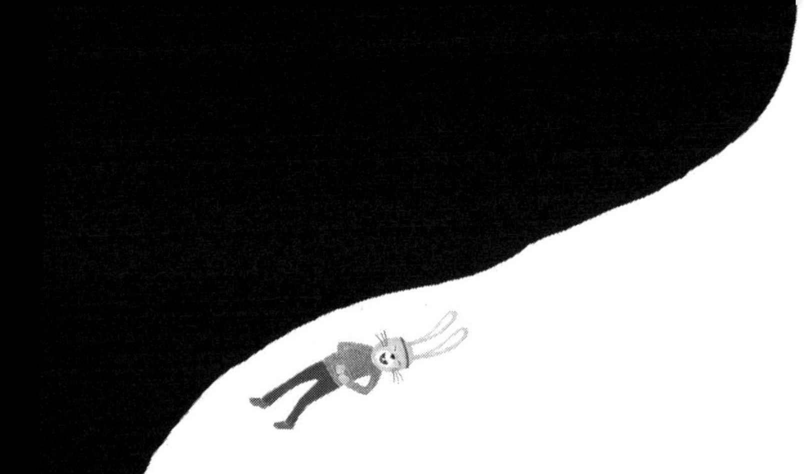

**27** OCTOBER

DID YOU KNOW THAT YOUR NOSE CAN RECOGNISE A GREAT NUMBER OF SMELLS? WE MAY NOT HAVE THE SENSE OF SMELL OF AN ELEPHANT OR A BLOODHOUND, BUT WE CAN REMEMBER UP TO 50,000 TYPES OF SCENT.

**28** OCTOBER

NO MATTER HOW MUCH YOU TELL MEN "LISTEN CAREFULLY TO WHAT I SAY", THEY WILL NEVER BE ABLE TO HEAR IT IN THE SAME WAY AS WOMEN. THIS IS BECAUSE MEN AND WOMEN HEAR DIFFERENTLY: MEN PROCESS SOUNDS WITH ONLY ONE SIDE OF THE TEMPORAL LOBE OF THE BRAIN, WHILE WOMEN USE BOTH.

**29** OCTOBER

DID YOU KNOW THAT MOST OF THE DUST IN YOUR HOUSE COMES FROM YOU? AS IMPOSSIBLE AS IT MAY SEEM, THOSE LITTLE SPECKS WE SEE WHEN WE OPEN THE WINDOWS AND ON OUR FURNITURE ARE MADE UP OF 90 PERCENT OF DEAD SKIN CELLS. IF WE SHED 300,000 TO 600,000 PARTICLES PER HOUR, IMAGINE HOW MUCH DUST WE CAN COLLECT IN A SINGLE DAY!

**30**
OCTOBER

IF OUR SOLAR SYSTEM IS ONLY A SMALL PART OF OUR GALAXY, THE MILKY WAY, THEN IMAGINE HOW ENORMOUS THE UNIVERSE IS, WHERE NASA ESTIMATES THAT THERE ARE BETWEEN 200 BILLION AND 2 TRILLION GALAXIES.

**31**
OCTOBER

WHO HAS MORE HAIR: BLONDES OR BRUNETTES? THIS QUESTION MAY SEEM SILLY, BUT THE TRUTH IS THAT BLONDES HAVE MORE HAIR, WITH AN AVERAGE OF 140,000 STRANDS OF HAIR, AS OPPOSED TO BRUNETTES WHO HAVE 110,000.

**01**
NOVEMBER

DID YOU KNOW THAT WE ARE TALLER WHEN WE WAKE UP? THIS IS TRUE. IF YOU MEASURE YOUR BODY IN THE MORNING YOU WILL FIND THAT IT IS 1 TO 2 CENTIMETRES (0.4 TO 0.78 INCHES) TALLER THAN IT IS AT NIGHT. THERE ARE DONUT-SHAPED DISCS BETWEEN THE VERTEBRAE IN YOUR SPINE THAT WORK LIKE SHOCK ABSORBERS TO HELP YOU MOVE. WHEN WE GET UP, THEY ARE TIGHTER BECAUSE THEY HAVE NOT BEEN UNDER THE PRESSURE OF GRAVITY, WHICH MEANS THAT WE ARE A LITTLE TALLER.

**02**
NOVEMBER

ALTHOUGH IT MAY SEEM LIKE A LOT OF FUN TO PRETEND TO BE KINGS AND QUEENS, IT ISN'T SO MUCH FUN IN REAL LIFE IF YOU ARE ONE AS A CHILD. IN THE UK, 3 KINGS WERE UNDER 10 YEARS OLD: EDWARD VI AND HENRY III WERE 9 YEARS OLD, WHILE HENRY VI WAS ONLY 8 MONTHS AND 25 DAYS OLD.

**03**
NOVEMBER

THERE ARE MILLIONS OF STONES FOUND IN THE GREAT PYRAMID OF EGYPT, ALMOST 2.5 MILLION OF THEM, WEIGHING FROM 2 TONS TO MORE THAN 50 TONS. AND THE MOST SURPRISING IS THAT MANY OF THE STONES WERE NOT WHERE THEY BUILT THE PYRAMID, BUT HAD TO GO TO COLLECT THEM... FROM MORE THAN 500 MILES AWAY!

**04**
NOVEMBER

CAN YOU TELL ME WHICH IS THE BIGGEST RIVER IN THE WORLD? FOR A REALLY LONG TIME IT WAS THOUGHT TO BE THE NILE RIVER... UNTIL SCIENTISTS WENT TO MEASURE THE AMAZON AND FOUND THAT THIS WAS ACTUALLY THE LARGEST RIVER IN THE WORLD.

**05**
NOVEMBER

IMAGINE WHAT IS IT LIKE WALKING AND MOVING AROUND THE ASPHALT OF A MOTORWAY. WELL, THIS IS HOW IT WOULD FEEL IF YOU WENT TO TORONTO'S YONGE STREET IN CANADA, THE LONGEST STREET IN THE WORLD AT 35 MILES LONG. NO WONDER IT WAS CALLED " HIGHWAY 11 " IN 1920.

**06**
NOVEMBER

WHEN I MENTION PYRAMIDS, YOU PROBABLY THINK OF EGYPT, BUT DID YOU KNOW THAT THERE ARE ALMOST TWICE AS MANY IN SUDAN? THEY ARE KNOWN AS THE NUBIAN PYRAMIDS AND THOUGH THEY ARE SMALLER, THERE ARE MORE THAN 250 PYRAMIDS BUILT ALONG THE NILE RIVER. HISTORIANS TELL US THAT THEY WERE BUILT FOR THE KUSHITE RULERS.

**07**
NOVEMBER

DID YOU KNOW THAT THE FIRST SOLAR CALENDAR IN HISTORY IS ALMOST 5,000 YEARS OLD? IT DID NOT HAVE MONTHS AND NUMBERS LIKE TODAY'S CALENDAR, BUT IT DID HAVE BEAUTIFUL DRAWINGS THAT THE EGYPTIANS MADE BY OBSERVING THE SKY AND THE FLOODS OF THE NILE RIVER. THEY WERE THE FIRST TO DISCOVER THE CYCLE OF THE YEAR, DIVIDING IT INTO 12 PARTS OF 30 DAYS. AT THE END OF THE LAST MONTH THEY ADDED 5 DAYS, CALLED EPAGOMENON, WHICH WERE NEEDED TO FINISH THE MONTH, DEDICATED TO 5 EGYPTIAN GODS.

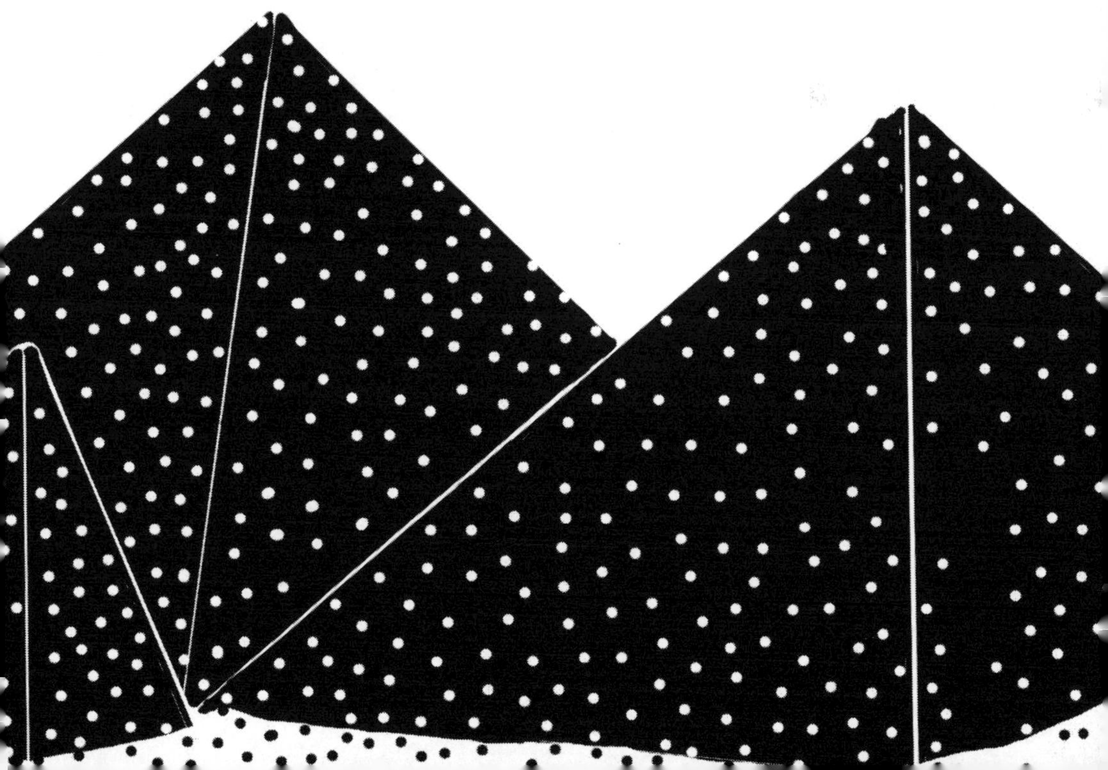

## 08 NOVEMBER

IF YOU EAT A SANDWICH ON THE BEACH YOU WILL PROBABLY END UP SHARING IT WITH PIGEONS OR SEAGULLS. BUT WHAT ABOUT IF INSTEAD OF THOSE BIRDS, IT WAS A GROUP OF HUNGRY PIGS? IT'S HARD TO IMAGINE, BUT THIS IS WHAT HAPPENS ON AN ISLAND CALLED "PIG BEACH" IN THE BAHAMAS, WHERE ONLY PIGS LIVE THERE AND DIVE INTO THE WATER LOOKING FOR FOOD BROUGHT IN BY TOURISTS.

## 09 NOVEMBER

IF YOU EVER TRAVEL TO THAILAND, REMEMBER THAT IT'S ALWAYS BETTER TO LAUGH AND NOT CRY. OTHERWISE, YOU MAY GET A SURPRISE VISIT FROM A BEE, A SPECIES THAT LIKES TO FEED ON... HUMAN TEARS!

## 10 NOVEMBER

CAN YOU IMAGINE AN EARTHWORM AS TALL AS AN ADULT PERSON? THE GIANT GIPPSLAND EARTHWORM IS LOCATED IN AUSTRALIA AND IT IS THE WORLD'S LARGEST AT 1.80 METRES (6 FEET) LONG.

## 11 NOVEMBER

FISH ARE NORMALLY FOUND SWIMMING IN THE WILD. BUT DID YOU KNOW THAT THEY ALSO FOUND A COFFEE SHOP? IN VIETNAM THERE IS A COFFEE SHOP THAT HAS ITS FLOOR COVERED WITH 25 CENTIMETRES (10 INCHES) OF WATER, WHERE JAPANESE CARP SWIM AROUND THE CUSTOMERS AS USUAL. WOULD YOU DARE TO PUT YOUR FEET IN THE WATER?

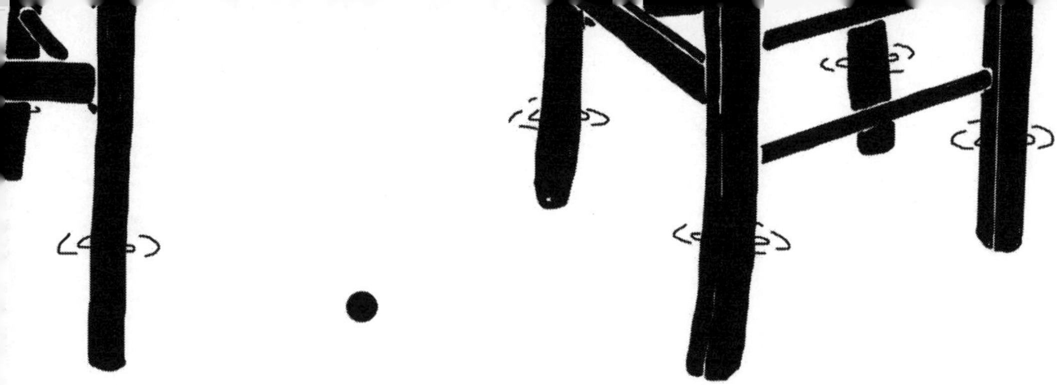

**12** NOVEMBER

THE MANDARIN FISH LOOKS LIKE THE CREATION OF AN AMAZING PAINTER, AND NOT ONLY BECAUSE OF ITS MAGICAL PATTERNS AND ITS BURST OF COLOUR. IN FACT, THIS IS THE ONLY TYPE OF VERTEBRATE CAPABLE OF PRODUCING BLUE PIGMENT IN THE PACIFIC OCEAN.

**13** NOVEMBER

HOW MANY THINGS COULD YOU DO AND LEARN IF YOU COULD LIVE 270 YEARS? WE'LL HAVE TO ASK THE GIANT ALDABRA TORTOISE, THE SECOND LARGEST TORTOISE IN THE WORLD AFTER THE GIANT GALAPAGOS TORTOISE. THEY CAN LIVE ALL THOSE YEARS, REACHING A LENGTH OF MORE THAN 1 METRE (3.2 FEET) AND WEIGHING UP TO 250 KILOS (550 POUNDS).

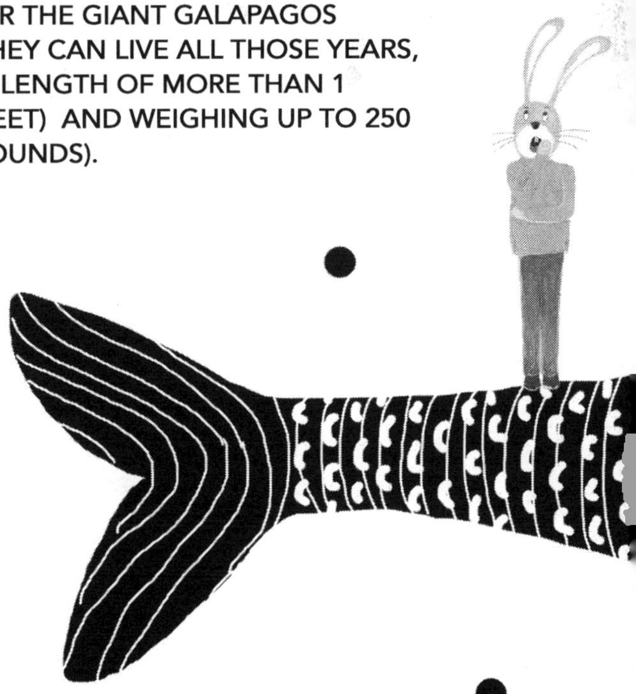

**14** NOVEMBER

IF YOU WANT SUNNY SUMMER DAYS TO LAST LONGER, YOU'LL HAVE TO TRAVEL TO FINLAND. A COUNTRY KNOWN AS THE LAND OF THE MIDNIGHT SUN, AS THE SUN STILL SHINES AT NIGHT FOR SOME MONTHS OF THE YEAR. A SINGLE SUMMER DAY CAN LAST MORE THAN TWO MONTHS THERE.

**15** NOVEMBER

DID YOU KNOW THAT IN SPAIN THERE IS A MAN WHO DEDICATED 60 YEARS OF HIS LIFE TO BUILDING A CATHEDRAL ALL BY HIMSELF? HIS NAME IS JUSTO GALLEGO AND HE DID IT WITHOUT ANY KNOWLEDGE OF ARCHITECTURE, USING ALL KINDS OF RECYCLED MATERIALS. HE DIED AT THE AGE OF 96 AND NEVER GOT TO SEE HIS CATHEDRAL COMPLETED.

**16** NOVEMBER

IF YOU LIVED IN RUSSIA, YOU WOULD HAVE TO CHOOSE WHERE YOU AND YOUR FRIENDS LIVE WISELY. RUSSIA IS SO BIG THAT IT HAS UP TO 11 TIME ZONES IN TOTAL, WHICH MEANS THAT WHILE YOU'RE WAKING UP AT ONE END OF THE COUNTRY, PEOPLE AT THE OTHER END ARE GOING TO SLEEP.

17
NOVEMBER

ONCE UPON A TIME THERE WAS A LITTLE ITALIAN VILLAGE CALLED VIGANELLA, SURROUNDED BY MOUNTAINS AND A FAKE SUN. YES, YOU READ THAT RIGHT! THE VILLAGERS FIGURED OUT A WAY TO GET THE HIDDEN SUNLIGHT BY PLACING A GIGANTIC 40-SQUARE METRE MIRROR ON TOP OF MOUNT SCAGLIOLA, AT ALMOST 1,000 METRES (3,280 FEET) ABOVE SEA LEVEL.

18
NOVEMBER

WOULD YOU BE ABLE TO LIVE IN TOTAL DARKNESS FOR 67 DAYS? THIS IS WHAT THE PEOPLE OF BARROW IN ALASKA EXPERIENCE WITH THE SUNLIGHT: THE SUN SETS ON 18 NOVEMBER AND DOESN'T RISE UNTIL 23 JANUARY.

19
NOVEMBER

THE SMALLEST COUNTRY IN THE WORLD HAS A POPULATION OF JUST 800 PEOPLE, BUT ALSO THE LARGEST COLLECTION OF WORKS OF ART ON THE PLANET. THIS IS VATICAN CITY, MEASURING LESS THAN HALF A SQUARE KILOMETRE.

20 NOVEMBER

IT IS AS TALL AS A 12-STOREY BUILDING AND AS HEAVY AS 15 ELEPHANTS PUT TOGETHER... FOR YOUR PEACE OF MIND, THIS GIANT IS NOT ALIVE ANYMORE... BUT IT WAS MANY YEARS AGO. THE SEISMOSAURUS WAS THE LARGEST DINOSAUR EVER DISCOVERED, STANDING MORE THAN 30 METRES TALL AND WEIGHING MORE THAN 80 TONNES.

21 NOVEMBER

SNAKES COME IN ALL SIZES AND COLOURS. SOME WON'T SCARE YOU SO MUCH AND OTHERS WILL HAVE YOU RUNNING FOR YOUR LIFE. THE SMALLEST SNAKE IN THE WORLD IS 10 CENTIMETRES (4 INCHES) IN SIZE AND THE LARGEST IS OVER 10 METRES (33 FEET) LONG.

22 NOVEMBER

THE WORLD'S LARGEST ANIMAL IS AS HEAVY AS 10 BUSES! THE BLUE WHALE CAN LIVE UP TO 100 YEARS OLD, MEASURE 30 METRES (98 FEET) LONG, AND WEIGH 199 TONNES (398,000 POUNDS).

23 NOVEMBER

CAN YOU IMAGINE SWIMMING UNDERWATER FOR MORE THAN 500 YEARS? WELL, THIS IS WHAT THE GREENLAND SHARK DOES, THE WORLD'S LONGEST-LIVING VERTEBRATE, WHICH CAN LIVE TO 512 YEARS OF AGE WITH AN AVERAGE LIFESPAN OF 272 YEARS.

24 NOVEMBER

IF YOU EVER ENCOUNTER A SHARK... ALWAYS RUN AWAY AS FAST AS POSSIBLE! UNLESS IT IS A DWARF SHARK, A HARMLESS SPECIES MEASURING LESS THAN 25 CENTIMETRES (10 INCHES).

25 NOVEMBER

WOULD YOU BE ABLE TO REMEMBER THE NAMES OF YOUR FUTURE CHILDREN... IF THERE WERE MORE THAN 500 OF THEM? YOU'LL HAVE TO ASK A RABBIT, WHO CAN HAVE UP TO 800 CHILDREN, GRANDCHILDREN, AND GREAT-GRANDCHILDREN IN ITS LIFETIME.

**26** NOVEMBER

CAN YOU IMAGINE A SCHOOL IN THE SHAPE OF A BOAT SAILING ON THE RIVER? THIS IS WHAT WAS CREATED FOR CHILDREN WHO WERE UNABLE TO GET TO SCHOOL IN BANGLADESH, A COUNTRY WHERE MORE THAN 58 DIFFERENT RIVERS FLOW INTO THE SEA.

**27** NOVEMBER

DID YOU KNOW THAT RUSSIA IS 115 TIMES BIGGER THAN BANGLADESH, BUT MORE PEOPLE LIVE IN BANGLADESH THAN IN RUSSIA?

**28** NOVEMBER

WHAT IS YOUR FAVOURITE SUBJECT? PLAYING CHESS! IT MAY SOUND STRANGE BUT THIS IS WHAT A CHILD COULD ANSWER IN ARMENIA, WHERE THEY ARE TAUGHT CHESS AS PART OF THEIR COMPULSORY EDUCATION FROM THE AGE OF 6.

**29**
**NOVEMBER**

CUBANS DON'T ONLY KNOW HOW TO DANCE SALSA… THEY ACTUALLY KNOW A LOT MORE! SO MUCH SO THAT THEY HAVE THE HIGHEST LITERACY RATE IN ALL OF LATIN AMERICA (OVER 99%), WITH EDUCATION THAT IS PUBLIC AND FREE FOR ALL, INCLUDING UNIVERSITY AND SCHOOL STATIONERY.

**30**
**NOVEMBER**

YOU SHOULD TAKE CARE OF PLANTS… IF YOU DON'T WANT THEM TO COMMIT SUICIDE! INCREDIBLE AS IT MAY SEEM, IT HAS BEEN PROVEN THAT SOME SPECIES OF PLANTS MAY COMMIT SUICIDE IF THEIR LIVING CONDITIONS ARE NOT GOOD.

**01**
**DECEMBER**

IF YOU WANT YOUR PLANTS TO BRIGHTEN YOUR DAY, CHOOSE A NICE MELODY FOR THEM! BELIEVE IT OR NOT, THEY ALSO HAVE THEIR OWN MUSICAL TASTES. SCIENTISTS TELL US THAT THEY CAN SENSE MUSIC AND IT IMPROVE THEIR GROWTH AS A RESULT… OR MAKE IT WORSE IF IT'S NOT THE BEST MUSIC FOR THEM!

02
DECEMBER

DID YOU KNOW THAT THE HOT DOG IS ACTUALLY A SAUSAGE DOG? THIS IS THE REAL TRANSLATION OF "DACHSHUND", AS THEY USED TO CALL IT IN GERMANY. LATER, WITH THE EMIGRATION OF THE 19TH CENTURY, THE DOG TRAVELLED TO THE UNITED STATES, AND AS THEY DIDN'T KNOW HOW TO PRONOUNCE IT, SO THEY DECIDED TO CALL IT THE "SAUSAGE DOG".

03
DECEMBER

ONCE UPON A TIME THERE WAS A FAMOUS AVOCADO THAT GREW SO BIG THAT IT BECAME AS BIG AS A HUGE MELON. AFTER GROWING IT FOR MORE THAN 10 MONTHS, THIS LED TO THE HAWAIIAN FAMILY THAT GREW IT BREAKING THE GUINNESS RECORD AS IT WEIGHED 2.5 KILOS (5.5 POUNDS).

04
DECEMBER

IF YOU EVER TRAVEL TO ITALY AND DECIDE TO STOP IN VACONE, YOU WILL BE ABLE TO EAT IN THE SMALLEST RESTAURANT IN THE WORLD! BUT YOU WILL HAVE TO CHOOSE YOUR PARTNER VERY CAREFULLY, AS YOU CAN ONLY CHOOSE ONE PERSON TO SIT WITH YOU, AT THE ONLY TABLE OF TWO IN THIS MINI DINING ROOM.

05
DECEMBER

IF YOU EVER TRAVEL TO RUSSIA AND WANT TO TRY THE REAL POTATO SALAD, YOU'RE GOING TO BE DISAPPOINTED IF YOU TRY CALLING IT "THE RUSSIAN POTATO SALAD". DESPITE ITS ORIGIN, THIS POPULAR DISH IS KNOWN THERE AS "OLIVIER POTATO SALAD", THE NAME OF THE CHEF WHO MADE IT SO FAMOUS.

06
DECEMBER

CAN YOU IMAGINE HAVING TO TRAVEL WITHOUT GETTING OUT OF YOUR CAR FOR 12 DAYS? HOW MANY SONGS AND GAMES WOULD YOU MAKE UP? THAT'S HOW LONG IT TOOK TO DRIVE 70 MILES (WHICH NORMALLY TAKES JUST 1 HOUR!) IN THE WORLD'S LONGEST TRAFFIC JAM. THIS TRAFFIC JAM HAPPENED IN AUGUST 2010, ON THE G110 HIGHWAY LINKING TIBET AND PEKING.

07
DECEMBER

DID YOU KNOW THAT SUGAR CANE GLOWS IN THE DARK? WHEN WE CRUSH IT, ITS CRYSTALS BREAK, AND WHEN THEIR MOLECULES COLLIDE THEY PRODUCE LIGHT. A PROCESS KNOWN AS "TRIBOLUMINESCENCE".

**08**
DECEMBER

MEN AND WOMEN ARE NOT ONLY DIFFERENT ON THE OUTSIDE... THEY ARE ALSO DIFFERENT ON THE INSIDE! TO MAKE A NEW BABY, WOMEN USE THE EGG, WHICH IS THE LARGEST CELL IN THEIR BODY. HOWEVER, MEN USE THEIR SMALLEST CELL, THE TINY SPERM THAT SWIMS A LONG JOURNEY TO JOIN THE EGG AND FERTILISE IT. SPERM CELLS ARE SO TINY THAT, UNLIKE THE EGG, OUR EYE COULD NOT SEE THEM.

**09**
DECEMBER

BY THE TIME YOU READ THIS SENTENCE, 500,000 CELLS IN YOUR BODY ARE GOING TO DIE... BUT YOUR BODY IS SO WISE, IT HAS ALREADY REPLACED THEM WITH 500,000 NEW ONES!

**10** DECEMBER

WE ARE MORE BACTERIA THAN WE THINK! OUR BODY HAS 10 TIMES MORE BACTERIA THAN HUMAN CELLS, WHICH IS UP TO 2 KILOS (4.4 POUNDS) OF OUR WEIGHT! BUT THE MAJORITY OF THEM ARE GOOD AND NECESSARY, WITH ONLY 1 IN 100 MAKING US SICK.

**11** DECEMBER

THANKS TO THEIR SKILLS, DOGS ARE DEFINITELY DETECTIVES. THEY HAVE A POWERFUL SENSE OF SMELL A THOUSAND TIMES BETTER THAN HUMANS AND ARE ABLE TO SENSE THE WORLD AROUND THEM.

**12** DECEMBER

CATERPILLARS ARE VERY SQUISHY, BUT DID YOU KNOW THAT THEY HAVE A LOT MORE MUSCLES THAN YOU? UP TO 6 TIMES MORE! THIS TINY ANIMAL HAS BETWEEN 2,000 AND 4,000 MUSCLES, UNLIKE HUMANS WHO ONLY HAVE 650.

**13** DECEMBER

DID YOU KNOW THAT CENTIPEDES DON'T ACTUALLY HAVE 100 LEGS? THEY RANGE FROM THE SMALLEST WITH ONLY 30 LEGS TO THE MOST GIGANTIC WALKING CENTIPEDES... WITH AS MANY AS 350! IMAGINE HOW LONG IT WOULD TAKE THEM TO TIE THEIR SHOELACES IF THEY HAD TO WEAR SHOES.

## 14 DECEMBER

DID YOU KNOW THAT ONE-FIFTH OF THE PLANET'S FRESHWATER COMES FROM ONE RIVER? IT'S THE AMAZON RIVER, WHICH RUNS THROUGH 3 COUNTRIES AND FORMS THE LARGEST RIVER DELTA IN THE WORLD. THIS IMMENSE RIVER IS SO LONG THAT IT PUMPS OUT MORE FRESH WATER THAN THE 7 LARGEST RIVERS COMBINED.

## 15 DECEMBER

IF YOU DREW A RIVER YOU WOULD PROBABLY FILL IT WITH COLOURFUL FISH, BUT YOU MIGHT ALSO FIND A LOT MORE LIFE IN THEM THAN YOU IMAGINE. THE MOST POPULATED IS THE AMAZON RIVER WITH THE GREATEST BIODIVERSITY IN THE WORLD: IT ALONE IS HOME TO ONE-THIRD OF ALL THE SPECIES THAT EXIST ON EARTH.

## 16 DECEMBER

TO BECOME A TRUE KING OF THE JUNGLE, YOU HAVE TO TRAVEL TO SURINAME OR MICRONESIA. THESE COUNTRIES HAVE HUGE FORESTS AND THICK JUNGLES, MAKING THEM THE ONLY TWO COUNTRIES IN THE WORLD WITH MORE THAN 90 PERCENT OF THEIR LAND COVERED BY ENDLESS JUNGLES.

**17**
DICIEMBRE

THE WORLD'S LARGEST WATERFALL IS NOT A SINGLE WATERFALL... IT ACTUALLY HAS BETWEEN 250 AND 350 WATERFALLS! THESE ARE THE IGUAZU FALLS, WHICH ARE LOCATED BETWEEN BRAZIL AND ARGENTINA.

**18**
DECEMBER

HOW ARE A CAMEL AND AN ANT SIMILAR? AT FIRST GLANCE, NOT AT ALL! BUT THESE LITTLE INSECTS CAN ALSO STORE WATER IN THEIR TINY BELLIES. ANTS GROW UP TO 1 CENTIMETRE TO BE ABLE TO FEED THEMSELVES AND IF THEY EVER GET HUNGRY THEY DRINK FROM OTHER ANTS' LIQUIDS.

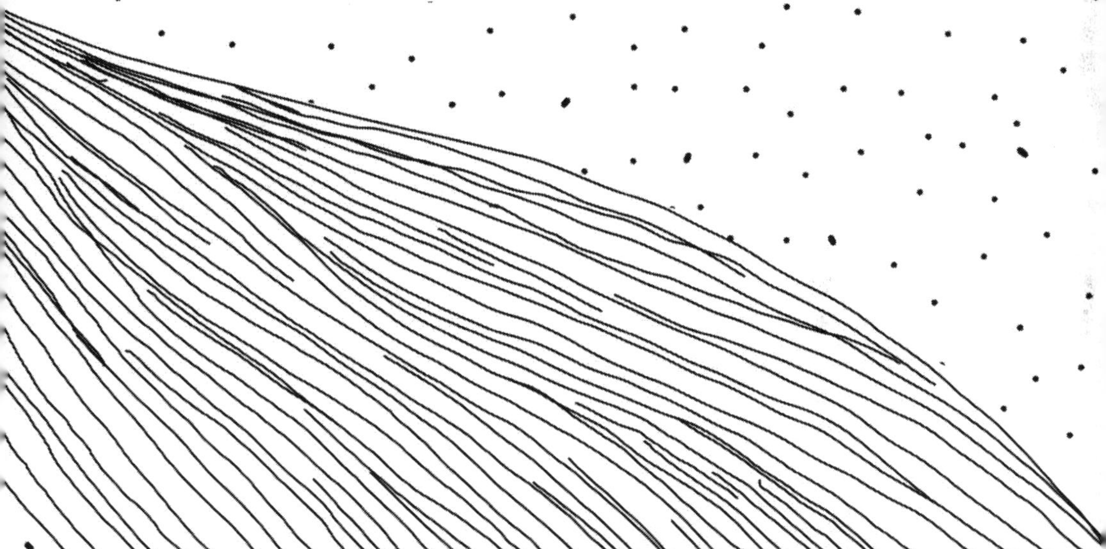

**19**
DECEMBER

DESPITE BEING SO BIG, YOU WILL NEVER BE ABLE TO SEE HOW MUCH THE TALLEST MOUNTAIN ON THE PLANET HAS GROWN... UNLESS YOU WEAR A GOOD PAIR OF DIVING GOGGLES BECAUSE MORE THAN HALF OF IT IS HIDDEN UNDERWATER. THE GREAT MAUNA KEA IS OVER 10,000 METRES (32,800 FEET) TALL AND 1,200 METRES (3,940 FEET) TALLER THAN MOUNT EVEREST.

20
DECEMBER

NEVER CUT A CAT'S WHISKERS, OR YOU COULD GIVE THEM A HARD TIME! THESE AREN'T JUST LITTLE HAIRS LIKE WHAT HUMANS HAVE: IF CATS LOSE THEM, THEY COULD FALL OVER AND BECOME CONFUSED, AS THEY USE THEM TO MEASURE DISTANCES AND DETECT MOVEMENT.

21
DECEMBER

THE WORLD'S MOST SLEEPY ANIMAL SPENDS ONLY 2 HOURS AWAKE AND 22 HOURS ASLEEP. THIS IS THE KOALA BEAR, EVEN LAZIER THAN THE SLOTH!

22
DECEMBER

IF PUT ON A DUCK'S BEAK, A BEAVER'S TAIL, AND OTTER'S FEET, YOU WILL HAVE DISGUISED YOURSELF AS A PLATYPUS! APART FROM THIS UNUSUAL APPEARANCE, THE PLATYPUS IS AN EGG-LAYING MAMMAL, AND DESPITE ITS CUTE APPEARANCE, IT CAN BE POISONOUS.

23 DECEMBER

DESPITE ITS BAD REPUTATION, THE MOST POISONOUS ANIMAL IN THE WORLD IS NOT A SNAKE... IT'S ACTUALLY A FROG! THESE AMPHIBIANS SEEM HARMLESS AND FRIENDLY TO US, BUT WE HAVE TO BE VERY CAREFUL WITH GOLDEN POISON DART FROGS! THEIR SKIN IS HIGHLY TOXIC AND IT CAN KILL 10 PEOPLE.

24 DECEMBER

THERE IS NO ANIMAL MORE SKILLED UNDERGROUND THAN A MOLE! IN A SINGLE NIGHT, THIS SKILLFUL ANIMAL CAN DIG A TUNNEL AS DEEP AS 100 METRES (330 FEET).

25 DECEMBER

CHRISTMAS IS INCREDIBLY MAGICAL... JUST TELL FATHER CHRISTMAS! HE IS ABLE TO GIVE GIFTS TO ALL THE CHILDREN IN THE WORLD - AND THERE ARE MORE THAN 2 BILLION OF THEM! HE ALONE MANAGES TO MAKE 842 MILLION VISITS IN A SINGLE NIGHT.

**26** DECEMBER

RUSSIA IS A COUNTRY SO HUGE THAT IT IS 70 TIMES THE SIZE OF THE UNITED KINGDOM AND IS EQUAL TO ONE-NINTH OF THE EARTH. WITH AN AREA OF 10.5 MILLION SQUARE MILES, IT IS THE LARGEST COUNTRY IN THE WORLD.

**27** DECEMBER

THE UNITED KINGDOM LOOKS VERY ISOLATED NOW, BUT DID YOU KNOW THAT THIS ANCIENT KINGDOM INVADED MANY OTHER COUNTRIES IN THE WORLD? IN FACT, ONLY 22 COUNTRIES WERE NOT INVADED BY THEM.

**28** DECEMBER

ALL OVER THE WORLD WE CALL PEOPLE WHO TRAVEL INTO SPACE ASTRONAUTS, EXCEPT IN RUSSIA WHERE THEY ARE CALLED COSMONAUTS, AS WELL AS IN CHINA WHERE THEY ARE CALLED TAIKONAUTS.

**29** DECEMBER

IF YOU WANT TO BE AN ASTRONAUT WHEN YOU GROW UP, REMEMBER THAT YOU CAN'T BURP IN SPACE. THE LACK OF GRAVITY CAUSES THE AIR, FOOD, AND LIQUIDS IN YOUR STOMACH TO FLOAT TOGETHER LIKE BUBBLES, SO IF YOU TRY TO BURP IN SPACE... YOU MIGHT JUST VOMIT IN YOUR MOUTH!

**30**
DECEMBER

IF YOU'VE EVER SEEN SNOW, YOU'RE A VERY LUCKY PERSON! AFTER ALL, THERE ARE VERY FEW PEOPLE WHO HAVE SEEN IT, ONLY 1 IN 3 PEOPLE IN THE WHOLE WORLD!

**31**
DECEMBER

IF YOU EVER LIVE IN HAWAII OR THE ISLANDS OF THE PACIFIC OCEAN, YOU WILL HAVE TO WAIT LONGER THAN ANYONE ELSE TO CELEBRATE NEW YEAR'S EVE. BECAUSE OF THEIR LOCATION, THE PEOPLE WHO LIVE THERE ARE THE LAST TO START THE NEW YEAR.

I'M SURE YOU KNOW MORE INTERESTING FACTS!

WRITE THEM IN THE FOLLOWING PAGES

# THE END

Printed in Poland
by Amazon Fulfillment
Poland Sp. z o.o., Wrocław
10 January 2023

b4ff9be8-9be7-47f6-9d20-59356365734bR01